Glorious
GRILLING!

Cover design by Knockout Books
Page design by Melanie Haage Design

Published in the United States of America by
Pascoe Publishing, Inc.
Rocklin, California
www.pascoepublishing.com

ISBN: 1-929862-24-5

TABLE OF CONTENTS

WELCOME TO GLORIOUS GRILLING!

Savor sweet-grilled vegetables. Delight in rich steaks and chops marinated to grilled perfection. Discover perfectly grilled fish and poultry. You'll find a wealth of superior recipes inside the pages of *Glorious Grilling!* MaryAnn and I use our grill during every season of the year and we believe that grilling brings family and friends together like no other method of cooking. The idea of a "family barbecue" or a "friendly barbecue get-together" brings to mind the images of grilled meats, grilled corn and sweet peppers, potato salads and special grilled desserts—enjoyed by people of all ages. After trying the recipes inside *Glorious Grilling!*, we hope you'll agree.

As you prepare the recipes in this cookbook, we hope you'll use your Ultrex® kitchen appliances, bakeware, cookware and accessories that have been designed for excellence. Visit us at www.hsn.com, keyword, "Ultrex," when you are looking for some exciting Ultrex pieces to add to your collection. We design all of our products with you—our best customers—in mind!

Art & MaryAnn Krull

CHAPTER ONE

INTRODUCTION

Have you ever stepped outside just as the day fades to dusk and catch the aroma of a backyard grill, fired up and ready to go? The smoke, the slightly sharp whiff of charcoal fluid and the lingering smell of a freshly burned match all combine to take you back to your best grilling memories. Surely experts must agree that one of the most primal and sensory aromas is that of a steak grilling in the backyard!

This cookbook is designed so that you can enjoy the versatility of your grill, whether it is an indoor or outdoor model and whether you prefer charcoal, electric or gas methods. Everyone has a favorite method and a sure-fire recipe and we've built on those recipes in *Glorious Grilling!* You'll find that each piece of beef, pork or lamb and every cut of chicken and turkey is supremely enhanced by the simple act of grilling. The quick heat of grilling is also perfect for fish and

1

shellfish, especially after the fish has been prepared in a delicate marinade.

Beyond the basic barbecue sauces and past the most obvious accompaniments for your grill, you'll find included in these pages a wide array of intriguing and satisfying grilling choices. Select from dinner entreés and grilled vegetables or salads, desserts and breads—foods of all kinds are meant for your grill! Don't hesitate to experiment with favorite foods and your grill. If your food has a texture or density that will hold up to the grill and can fit on the grids of the grill or can be prepared on a barbecue rack or tray, chances are that food can be grilled to perfection.

The grilling times given for all of the recipes in *Glorious Grilling!* are approximate because many factors affect your actual grilling times. You'll find that weather makes a big difference as you grill and the type of briquets, wood chips or other radiant materials can change the timing of grilling. If you are using an indirect method of grilling, you'll also need to increase the time for grilling. After using your grill for a while, you'll become adjusted to the length of time needed for most recipes.

In this cookbook you'll find specific directions for indoor contact grills, charcoal grills and gas grills. Most other types of grills will include special instructions for specific models, but we've found these three types of grills to be most common. Always refer to your manufacturer's instructions when using your grill. Unique features and special safety issues will determine your grilling requirements.

Grilling is one of the most popular forms of cooking all around the world. From a simple hibachi-style grill to a massive grill big enough to hold an entire pig, the flavors of the grill are enjoyed universally with great delight. When you next catch that aroma of a grill, fired up and ready to go, reach for even the most simple ingredients and make your evening meal a special one.

■ = charcoal grill

■ = gas grill

■ = indoor contact grill

CHAPTER TWO

GRILLING BASICS:

INDOORS OR OUTDOORS, CHARCOAL OR GAS—ALL YOU NEED TO KNOW ABOUT GLORIOUS GRILLING!

All too often I watch someone overload a charcoal grill with briquets, light a fire that shoots to the sky and quickly throw a tender cut of beef onto the grill, even as the flames are licking beyond the top of the grill. Without a doubt, this is a recipe for disaster! There are some fairly simple and obvious steps to grilling perfection. In this chapter, we will quickly sketch out the various kinds of grills, tools that are handy for grilling and the methods best suited to grilling a variety of foods. In order to start, however, we must begin with the food that is to be grilled.

Choosing Your Foods: The Basics

In order to have good grilling results, you need to start with high-quality, fresh cuts of beef, pork and lamb. Chicken should be fresh or flash-frozen and thawed in the refrigerator for no more than a few hours. Fish should be as fresh as you can find it and preferably prepared the day it is purchased or caught. Shellfish should be fresh and cleaned properly. Vegetables need to carry solid textures and good density. Fruit should be ripe and without blemishes.

The quality of your food directly affects the outcome of your grilled foods. Why? Grilling is designed to quickly and efficiently cook foods over direct or indirect heat. Unlike an oven, where hot air is forced around the walls of the oven constantly, grilling heat has one source. Grilled foods must interact with the heat within minutes (unless you are smoking fish or beef, etc.), so the time allotted for grilling is necessarily short. For example, an oven-baked beef roast bakes for several hours. During that time the texture of the beef changes as the connective tissue breaks down in the meat. With the addition of liquid, the beef changes even more as it becomes tender. When grilling, by contrast, the cook has one source of heat and a fairly short window of time within which to grill, so the foods must be of premium quality to begin with. Start with the finest of ingredients and you will appreciate the results.

Choosing Your Grill: The Basics

There are more grills on the market today than ever before due to the growing popularity of grilling. When shopping for a grill, you will find small tabletop models and hibachi-style grills and you can find complete gourmet grilling islands with sale prices of several thousand dollars!

The bottom line is that you should select the grill that's right for you. If you are renting an apartment or have little or no outdoor space, a simple solution is the indoor grill. If you enjoy the rituals that go with preparing and lighting an outdoor grill and want the taste of true charcoal flavor, a charcoal grill may be your first choice. If you value the convenience and consistency that gas grills offer, you will want to look at the many models available. Let's look at each of the types of grills and the pros and cons of each.

INDOOR GRILLS

There are several basic models of indoor grills, along with combinations and specialty features of each. Without describing each of the unique models in depth, we will take a quick look at the most popular models of indoor grills: open hearth-style indoor grills, infusion grills and two-sided contact grills.

Open hearth grills offer the advantage of even and consistent heat, just as you would expect from an oven or stove burner. They are often coated with nonstick plating and can be fairly easy to clean. Heating elements are usually covered, which means that the fat and juices from grilling will collect underneath the grill, but will not splatter or cause smoke because the element never has direct contact with any food or liquid. The disadvantage of this type of grill is that foods typically require more time to cook than they would in a charcoal or gas grill that has a lid or a two-sided contact grill with a lid. Open hearth indoor grills may or may not require preheating and often come with special cooling down instructions, as well.

Infusion grills are a more complex type of indoor grill that can be used for a variety of gourmet grilled dishes. The best infusion grills come with lids for steaming foods and can both grill foods on the nonstick plates as well as provide moisture via a fusion cup to tenderize or flavor foods as they grill. Infusion grills are typically more expensive than standard indoor grills and require more attention in care and clean-up.

Two-sided contact grills typically have nonstick plates with grooves that provide a "grilled" look to foods. Models range in size and price from very small, barely large enough for two hamburger patties, to very large, with enough grill space for 12 or more hamburger patties. The two-sided contact grills offer a couple of solid advantages over other indoor grills. Foods grill very quickly because the heat comes from both the upper plate and the lower plate. In fact, foods may grill more quickly in a two-sided contact grill than in any other type of grill available. When using a two-sided grill, you'll want to watch your food carefully to avoid overcooking. Clean-up is also relatively easy when using a two-sided contact grill indoors. Meat juices and grease run into small saucers below the grill and can be discarded easily. The natural splattering that occurs when meats and poultry first hit the grill is eliminated because the upper grill controls any splatters—adding another nice feature when it comes time to clean up.

CHARCOAL GRILLS

Although charcoal grills can be the least expensive of the standing grill models, they can also range in price up to several hundred dollars, especially if you are looking for added features and larger sizes of grilling space. A standard, lower-end standing charcoal grill is typically available for about $30 to 40 and that is a great price for grilling heaven! However, depending on the size of your family and how often you plan to grill, you may want to consider making a more expensive purchase as a long-term type of investment in great taste.

Charcoal grills have been used for many generations in this country. When using a charcoal grill, you must have at hand the briquets and lighter fluid or lighting element that is required. Nothing is worse than getting everything ready to grill and discovering that you have no briquets!

The best charcoal grills have an ash receptacle that makes emptying the grill far less of a chore than the basic models that require scooping out the ashes once a week. Look for models that offer this important today and your choices will depend on the foods you grill. Look for high-quality, heat-resistant trays, grids and baskets and look for easy-to-clean features throughout.

METAL & BAMBOO SKEWERS

Kebobs of all kinds are especially flavorful when prepared on the grill. You may choose metal skewers of medium to long length or bamboo skewers that are short to medium length. Either way, the results are the same. The bamboo skewers should always be soaked in water for at least 10 minutes and drained before using. This prevents the bamboo from burning while on the grill.

WOOD CHIPS

As any true grilling gourmet will say, the delight of grilled foods is in the smoky flavor imparted from the grill. Wood chips carry that smoky flavor, depending on the type of wood used. For example, salmon is often paired with alder wood in the Pacific Northwest and hickory is a partner to pork in the South. The easiest way to use wood chips is to add them slowly and in small quantities to a fire that is already established. Wood chips can be added to a gas grill, however they should be contained in a smoker box or other accessory so that they don't actually catch fire. Refer to your manufacturer's instructions to determine how wood chips work best with your grill.

Once you have mastered the basics of grilling and feel comfortable with some new directions, try sweet wood chips such as apple and maple for pork or ham and mesquite wood chips for any Southwestern-flavored foods—you will be delighted with the results!

Choosing Your Grilling Method: The Basics

INDOOR CONTACT GRILLS

There are a few simple rules to keep in mind when using your contact grill. Although the grills usually have nonstick plates, it is best to spray the grids with cooking spray. This helps when it comes time to clean up and keeps the nonstick surfaces in good shape. You should always preheat the grill for 5 minutes. If your grill has a variable temperature control, you will want to preheat the grill on medium-high heat.

Never use metal knives or forks inside the contact grill. Use a plastic spatula or fork to place and remove foods from your grill. Clean the grill as recommended by the manufacturer without using steel wool or other harsh abrasives.

Foods grill *very* quickly in a contact grill, so quickly, in fact, that you may find you've overcooked your food before you think about testing it. Watch your foods carefully when you first use your grill to determine the length of time needed for your favorite foods. Set the timer for 1 minute earlier than the suggested times. It's always better to continue grilling after the first test than to have overcooked food.

CHARCOAL GRILLS

To start your grill, mound briquets in the bottom of your grill. The grill should be free of ashes and the grids should be clean. *It is very important to use enough briquets to build an adequate fire for the amount of food you will grill.* Have you ever observed someone who prepares only a handful of briquets in the grill in a misguided attempt to save money with the sad result being a poorly grilled cut of beef or chicken at the table? It's not a pretty thing!

The best beginning for your grill will also be the best presentation of your grilled foods. Use an adequate or even generous amount of briquets when starting the fire. Don't skimp in the name of economy.

Although starter fluid is a popular tool for starting charcoal fires, a new and safer option is the electric element starter. The element sits in the cold briquets for a short time, heating them to ash without causing direct flames and can be reused as often as needed. Whether you use fluid or an electric element, be sure to watch your grill during this time. You'll especially want to check for flames that are out of control.

After preparing your briquets, wait for them to heat to ash. They should be uniformly hot and glowing. Spread the briquets around the bottom of the grill to cover the area you'll need for grilling your foods. Allow a 1 to 2 inch margin wider in space than what you expect to actually use. It's preferable to have layers of briquets 2 deep to ensure even heating, especially if you will be grilling a

❖❖❖❖❖❖❖❖❖❖❖❖❖❖❖❖❖❖❖❖❖❖❖❖❖❖❖❖❖❖❖❖❖❖❖❖❖❖❖

large piece of meat or a whole turkey or chicken.

When you have removed your foods from the grill, you may scatter the briquets to cool them more quickly. Place the lid on your grill and let the grill cool slowly. Do not remove the ashes until they are completely dead and cold.

GAS GRILLS

With the clean grilling provided by gas, the most important task you will have is to properly heat the grill in preparation. You should *always* preheat the grill for 10 to 15 minutes on high heat before placing any food on the grill. This tempers the grill and raises the heat enough to start cooking the food the minute it hits the grids.

In order to grill by direct heat, reduce the heat to medium after preheating and place the food evenly on the grill. Close the lid and watch and test the food as needed. The recipes in this cookbook are only approximate, as many factors will affect your actual grilling times.

If you choose to grill by the indirect method, preheat the grill as usual. Turn off 1 burner and reduce the remaining burner(s) to medium. Place the food over the burner that is off and allow the foods to grill indirectly by using the heat from the other burner(s). This is a popular method when using gas grills because you have excellent control over the cooking time and foods that are delicate to grill can be easily tended. You may want to place a drip pan (with some water in it) under the food to catch the grease or juices from your foods.

❖❖❖❖❖❖❖❖❖❖❖❖❖❖❖❖❖❖❖❖❖❖❖❖❖❖❖❖❖❖❖❖❖❖❖❖❖❖❖

Pepper-Drenched Tri-Tip Roast

The fiery taste of peppers is sweetened and softened by the time spent marinating.

◆ ◆ ◆

2 1/2 – 3 pounds tri-tip roast

3/4 cup soy sauce

3/4 cup red wine vinegar

1/4 cup extra virgin olive oil

2 tablespoons Dijon mustard

4 cloves garlic, minced

1 teaspoon freshly ground black pepper

3 fresh Habañero peppers, finely minced

4 fresh Tabasco peppers, finely minced

◆ ◆ ◆

Place the roast in a large self-sealing plastic bag. Add the remaining ingredients and seal tightly. Refrigerate for up to 12 hours. Grill as directed. To serve, slice thinly across the grain and place on a heated serving platter. Serves 6–8.

C Grill over medium coals for 25 minutes. Turn, baste with the marinade and grill for 20 minutes, or until grilled as desired.

G Preheat the grill for 10 to 15 minutes on high heat. Turn off 1 burner and reduce the heat to medium on the remaining burner(s). Place the roast over the burner that is turned off. Close the lid and grill until cooked to your preference, about 60–80 minutes.

Sirloin Steaks with Rosemary Mustard Butter

Smooth herbed butter is an intriguing complement to these rich sirloin steaks.

◆ ◆ ◆

6 sirloin steaks, 3/4 to 1-inch thick

1/4 cup unsalted butter

2 teaspoons prepared yellow mustard

1 teaspoon ground paprika

1 tablespoon fresh rosemary, finely minced

1 teaspoon salt

1 teaspoon freshly ground black pepper

◆ ◆ ◆

Pat the steaks dry with paper toweling. Mix together the butter, mustard, paprika, rosemary, salt and pepper. Blend well. Place equal amounts of the butter on one side of each steak and smooth over the steaks evenly. Grill as directed. Serves 6.

C Grill over medium coals, buttered side facing up, for 7 minutes. Turn and grill for 5–7 minutes, or until cooked as desired.

G Preheat the grill for 10 to 15 minutes on high heat. Place the steaks directly on the burners and sear them for 1 minute. Turn 1 burner off and turn the remaining burner(s) to medium. Place the steaks over the burner that is off. Close the lid and grill for 14 to 16 minutes, or until cooked to your preference.

I Preheat the contact grill for 5 minutes. Grill, buttered side facing up, for 8 to 9 minutes, or until grilled as desired.

Grilled Red Pepper Beef Kebobs

Skirt steak is very thin and tender when grilled in this kebob recipe. If you have hungry diners, try doubling the portions because these will disappear quickly.

◆ ◆ ◆

1 1/2 – 2 pounds beef skirt steak, unwound and cut into 6 equal portions

3 tablespoons red wine vinegar

1/2 cup extra virgin olive oil

1 teaspoon salt

1 teaspoon freshly ground black pepper

1 teaspoon dry mustard

6 shallots, peeled and cut into quarters

2 red bell peppers, cored, seeded and cut into large pieces

6 10-inch bamboo skewers, soaked in water and drained

◆ ◆ ◆

Place the strips of steak in a large, self-sealing plastic bag. Add the vinegar, oil, salt, pepper and mustard and mix in the bag with the steak. Refrigerate for one hour. Discard the marinade, reserving ¼ cup. Thread the beef onto the skewers, wrapping the beef over and around the shallots and red pepper pieces on each skewer. Grill as directed. Serves 6.

C Grill the kebobs over medium coals for 6 minutes. Turn and baste with the reserved marinade. Grill for 4-6 minutes, or until grilled as desired.

G Preheat the grill for 10 to 15 minutes on high heat. Turn the burners to medium, place the skewers on the grill and cook for about 10 to 12 minutes, turning once or twice.

I Preheat the contact grill to medium heat. Place the kebobs evenly in the grill and cook for 7 to 8 minutes. Check for doneness and continue grilling as desired.

◆◆◆◆◆◆◆◆◆◆◆◆◆◆◆◆◆◆◆◆◆◆◆◆◆◆◆◆◆◆◆◆◆◆◆◆◆

Onion & Roasted Green Chile Sirloin Burgers

Prepare these hamburgers using high-quality sirloin for a truly delicious treat!

◆ ◆ ◆

1/2 cup purple onion, finely chopped

3 tablespoons roasted green chilies, chopped

1 teaspoon salt

1 teaspoon freshly ground black pepper

1/4 teaspoon Tabasco sauce

1 1/2 pounds beef ground sirloin

◆ ◆ ◆

◆◆◆◆◆◆◆◆◆◆◆◆◆◆◆◆◆◆◆◆◆◆◆◆◆◆◆◆◆◆◆◆◆◆◆◆◆

◆◆◆◆◆◆◆◆◆◆◆◆◆◆◆◆◆◆◆◆◆◆◆◆◆◆◆◆◆◆◆◆

Combine all of the ingredients except the ground sirloin in a medium bowl and toss to mix well. Add the ground sirloin and gently toss for two minutes with the other ingredients. Do not overmix or the beef will become tough. Lightly pat the beef into four patties, each about ¾ to 1-inch thick. Grill as directed. Serve on toasted sourdough bread with your choice of condiments. Serves 4.

C Grill over medium coals for 4 minutes. Turn once and grill for 5 to 6 minutes, or until grilled as desired.

G Preheat the grill for 15 minutes on high heat. Turn all burners to medium and grill the burgers over the burners for 4 to 5 minutes on each side, or until cooked as desired. Turn the burgers once while grilling.

I Preheat the contact grill to medium heat. Grill for 4 to 5 minutes, or until cooked as desired.

◆◆◆◆◆◆◆◆◆◆◆◆◆◆◆◆◆◆◆◆◆◆◆◆◆◆◆◆◆◆◆◆

Worcestershire & Lemon Marinated Top Sirloin

The tart and tangy combination of lemon and Worcestershire sauce makes the most delicious marinade! Try this marinade over any cut of beef for exceptional flavor.

◆ ◆ ◆

1 1/2 pounds beef top sirloin

1/2 cup vegetable oil

1/4 cup soy sauce

1/4 cup Worcestershire sauce

1/4 cup fresh lemon juice

1 teaspoon dry mustard

1 teaspoon salt

1 teaspoon freshly ground black pepper

2 tablespoons fresh parsley, minced

2 cloves garlic, minced

◆ ◆ ◆

Place the beef in a large, self-sealing plastic bag. Add the remaining ingredients and mix well. Refrigerate overnight. Discard the marinade and grill as directed. Serves 4–5.

Grill the sirloin over medium coals for 4 minutes. Turn and grill for 5–6 minutes, or until grilled as desired.

Preheat the grill for 10 to 15 minutes on high heat. Place the sirloin directly on the burners and sear it for 2 minutes. Turn 1 burner off and reduce the heat to medium on the remaining burner(s). Place the sirloin over the burner that is off. Close the lid and grill for 10 to 12 minutes, or until cooked to your preference.

Preheat the grill to medium heat. Grill for 5–6 minutes, or until cooked as desired.

Pepper-Crusted London Broil with Fresh Tomato Relish

London broil is a less-tender, lower-fat cut of beef that should be grilled to a rare or medium degree for best results. This fresh tomato relish partners readily with the grilled beef.

❖ ❖ ❖

3 large ripe tomatoes, chopped

2 cloves garlic, minced

1 cup canned or frozen and thawed whole kernel corn

1 small, white onion, chopped

2 teaspoons fresh cilantro, minced

1 tablespoon tomato sauce

1/2 teaspoon freshly ground black pepper

1 teaspoon salt

1 1/2 to 2 pounds beef London broil, 1 1/2 to 2 inches thick

2 to 3 tablespoons cracked black peppercorns

❖ ❖ ❖

Place the tomatoes, garlic, corn, onion and cilantro in a food processor and pulse once or twice briefly. Do not over-process. Place the vegetables in a medium bowl and add the tomato sauce, pepper and salt. Mix lightly and refrigerate while grilling the beef.

Prepare the beef for grilling by sprinkling the peppercorns over the surface of each side of the beef. Press the pepper securely into the beef. Grill as directed. Slice thinly to serve and pass the tomato relish on the side. Serves 4–6.

C Grill the London broil over medium coals for 8 minutes. Turn and continue grilling for 7–10 minutes, or according to your preference. The beef should be rare to medium for best results.

G Preheat the grill for 15 minutes on high heat. Place the steak directly over the burners and close the lid. Grill for 4 minutes. Turn 1 burner off and turn the remaining burner(s) to medium. Turn the steak and move it over the burner that is off. Close the lid and grill the steak for 13 to 15 minutes, turning once.

I Preheat the contact grill to medium. Grill the beef for 5 minutes. Turn halfway around on the grill to cook with the grids at right angles. Grill for 4–5 minutes, or until cooked to your preference.

Kansas City Rubbed Beef Tenderloin

This rub takes only a few minutes to make and offers superior flavor to grilled beef. Save any remaining rub in the refrigerator for up to 4 weeks.

◆ ◆ ◆

2 pounds beef tenderloin, cut into 6 portions

1/4 cup sugar

2 tablespoons salt

1 tablespoon ground paprika

1 teaspoon cayenne pepper

2 teaspoons chili powder

1 teaspoon ground cumin

◆ ◆ ◆

Place the beef on a flat surface. Mix the remaining ingredients together in a small plastic bag. Rub the spices into each side of the tenderloin pieces, pressing lightly to integrate the spices into the meat. Grill as directed. Serves 6.

Grill the tenderloin over medium coals for 6 minutes. Turn and grill for 5 to7 minutes, or until grilled to your preference.

Preheat the grill for 10 to 15 minutes on high heat. Place the steaks directly on the burners and sear them for 1 minute. Turn 1 burner off and turn the remaining burner(s) to medium. Place the steak over the burner that is off. Close the lid and grill for 12 to 14 minutes, or until cooked to your preference.

Preheat the grill to medium. Grill the beef for 8 to 10 minutes, or until cooked to your preference.

Blue Ribbon Barbecued Beef Ribs

Everyone needs a "blue ribbon" recipe for no-fail ribs and this is my favorite. Make sure there are plenty of napkins available when these spectacular ribs come to the table!

◆ ◆ ◆

1 tablespoon vegetable oil

1 purple onion, finely diced

8 ounce can tomato sauce

1/2 cup dark brown sugar

1/4 cup apple cider vinegar

2 tablespoons Worcestershire sauce

1/4 cup chili powder

1 teaspoon salt

1/2 teaspoon dry mustard

4 pounds beef ribs, trimmed of excess fat

◆ ◆ ◆

Sauté the onion for two to three minutes in the oil in a medium saucepan. Add the tomato sauce, brown sugar, vinegar, Worcestershire sauce, chili powder, salt and mustard. Blend well and cook and stir over medium-high heat until the sauce boils. Reduce the heat and simmer for 15 minutes. Cool slightly. Grill as directed, basting the ribs with the sauce. If desired, you may reheat any remaining sauce to boiling, simmer for 5 minutes and use at the table as a mop sauce for the ribs. Serves 4.

C Grill the ribs over medium coals for 4 minutes. Turn and brown the other side of the ribs for 2 minutes. Turn again and baste with the sauce, grilling for 6 minutes. Turn, baste and grill for 3–5 minutes. Test for doneness and continue basting and grilling until the ribs are cooked as desired.

G Preheat the grill for 10 to 15 minutes on high heat. Turn 1 burner off and reduce the heat to medium on the remaining burner(s). Place the ribs over the burner that is off. Close the lid and grill for about 18 to 25 minutes, turning the ribs and basting with the sauce occasionally.

Asian Chili Sauce Flank Steak

*Asian spice and soy sauce imbues this steak
with excellent flavor. Slicing the steak thinly
across the grain enhances the flavor and
tenderness of this cut of beef.*

◆ ◆ ◆

1 1/2 pounds beef flank steak, trimmed of
   any excess fat

3/4 cup vegetable oil

1/4 cup soy sauce

2 green onions, minced

2 cloves garlic, minced

1 teaspoon ground ginger

1 teaspoon Asian chili sauce

1 teaspoon freshly ground black pepper

1 teaspoon honey

◆ ◆ ◆

❖❖

Score the flank steak lightly in a two-inch diamond pattern to allow the marinade to penetrate the meat. Place the remaining ingredients in a large, self-sealing plastic bag and mix well. Add the beef and refrigerate for 4 to 12 hours. Discard the marinade and grill as directed. To serve, slice thinly across the grain of the meat. Serves 4–6.

C Grill the steak over medium coals for 8 minutes. Turn and grill for 10 to 14 minutes, or until cooked as desired.

G Preheat the grill for 10 to 15 minutes on high heat. Sear the steak on each side for 2 minutes. Turn off 1 burner and reduce the heat on the remaining burner(s) to medium. Move the steak over the burner that is off, close the lid and grill for 25 to 30 minutes, or until cooked to your preference.

I Preheat the contact grill for 5 minutes. Grill for 8–10 minutes, or until grilled as desired.

❖❖

INVITING GRILLED PORK & LAMB!

Jalapeño & Honeyed Pork Ribs

Asian Pork Tenderloin

Pork Chops in Midnight Marinade

Honey Mustard Pork Loin Chops

Smokin' Hot Rubbed Pork Loin Chops

Tender Greek Pork Kebobs

Gazpacho Pork Chops with Grilled Corn Salsa

Mediterranean Lamb Burgers

Grilled & Butterflied Lemon Leg of Lamb

Moroccan Lamb Shish Kebobs

Garlic & Rosemary Butterflied Leg of Lamb

Red Pepper-Rubbed Lamb Chops

Gold Tequila & Chile Lamb Kebobs

Dark & Sweet Molasses Lamb

◆◆◆◆◆◆◆◆◆◆◆◆◆◆◆◆◆◆◆◆◆◆◆◆◆◆◆◆◆◆◆◆◆◆◆◆

Introduction

Pork and lamb have the distinct advantages of excellent texture and mild flavor when it comes to grilling. You'll find in this chapter outstanding recipes for all kinds of special touches for pork and lamb, as well as a number of exciting dishes from around the world. For a refreshing change of pace, try *Jalapeño & Honeyed Pork Ribs, Pork Chops in Midnight Marinade, Smokin' Hot Rubbed Pork Loin Chops* and *Moroccan Lamb Shish Kebobs.*

In years past, cooking pork thoroughly was a serious issue because of bacteria-borne diseases. As pork production in recent years has eliminated some of those fears, you now have the choice to grill pork to medium or medium-well temperatures for a moist and tender grilled entrée. This is based strictly on your preference and it is important to keep your meat thermometer handy for accurate temperature readings. Marinades and sauces help to produce tender grilled pork and *Asian Pork Tenderloin* is an example of pork tenderly grilled to perfection.

Leg of lamb and lamb chops are flavorful and tender without any additional flavorings or marinades. A light dusting of garlic and pepper is just about all you need to produce excellent grilled lamb. However, when you want to serve a special meal, try *Grilled & Butterflied Lemon Leg of Lamb* or *Gold Tequila & Chile Lamb Kebobs.* You won't be disappointed in the lovely results.

◆◆◆◆◆◆◆◆◆◆◆◆◆◆◆◆◆◆◆◆◆◆◆◆◆◆◆◆◆◆◆◆◆◆◆◆

◆◆◆◆◆◆◆◆◆◆◆◆◆◆◆◆◆◆◆◆◆◆◆◆◆◆◆◆◆◆◆◆

Jalapeño & Honeyed Pork Ribs

These pork ribs pack a delightful punch!

◆ ◆ ◆

3 pounds pork ribs

1/4 cup jalapeño chile pepper, finely
   minced

1/2 cup soy sauce

2 cups prepared mild salsa

2 cloves garlic, minced

1/2 cup honey

◆ ◆ ◆

◆◆◆◆◆◆◆◆◆◆◆◆◆◆◆◆◆◆◆◆◆◆◆◆◆◆◆◆◆◆◆◆

Parboil the ribs by placing them in a large pot of boiling water. Reduce the heat and simmer for one hour. Remove the ribs from the water and place the ribs in a shallow glass baking dish. Mix together the chile pepper, soy sauce, salsa, garlic and honey and pour the sauce over the ribs. Cover the ribs tightly with plastic wrap and refrigerate for at least one hour or up to twelve hours. Turn the ribs occasionally in the marinade. Discard the marinade and grill as directed. Serves 4–6.

C Grill the ribs over medium coals for 10 minutes. Turn and grill for 10 to 20 minutes, or until grilled to your desire.

G Preheat the grill for 10 to 15 minutes on high heat. Turn 1 burner off and reduce the heat to medium on the remaining burner(s). Place the ribs over the burner that is off and close the lid. Grill the ribs for 1½ to 1¾ hours, basting occasionally.

Pork Chops in Midnight Marinade

*This dark, intense and inviting marinade
calls for tender pork chops. Add rice pilaf and a
lightly dressed green salad for an exotic meal.*

❖ ❖ ❖

3 tablespoons Worcestershire sauce

1/2 cup dry white wine

2 tablespoons extra virgin olive oil

1 teaspoon salt

1 teaspoon freshly ground black pepper

2 teaspoons hot chili sauce

1 tablespoon apple cider vinegar

3 tablespoons soy sauce

1/4 cup dark brown sugar

4 pork loin chops, 6 to 8 ounces each

❖ ❖ ❖

Combine all of the ingredients except for the pork chops in a large, self-sealing plastic bag. Mix thoroughly. Add the pork chops and marinate in the refrigerator for 2 hours or up to 12 hours. Remove the chops from the bag and grill as directed. Serves 4.

C Grill the chops over medium coals for 5 to 6 minutes. Turn and baste with the marinade. Grill for 4 to 5 minutes, or until cooked to your preference.

G Preheat the grill for 10 to 15 minutes on high heat. Turn off 1 burner and turn the remaining burner(s) to medium. Place the chops on the burner that is off and grill for 13 to 20 minutes, or according to your preference.

I Preheat the contact grill on medium for 5 minutes. Grill the chops for 6–8 minutes, or until cooked as desired.

Honey Mustard Pork Loin Chops

*Tangy mustard and sweet honey combine
with delectable results.*

◆ ◆ ◆

6 pork loin chops, 6 to 8 ounces each

3 tablespoons prepared Dijon mustard

1/4 cup clover honey

2 tablespoons lime juice

1/4 cup vegetable oil

1/4 teaspoon salt

1 teaspoon freshly ground pepper

1 tablespoon fresh parsley, minced

◆ ◆ ◆

Place the pork chops in a large, self-sealing plastic bag. Add the remaining ingredients and mix well, covering the chops completely. Refrigerate for 4 to 12 hours, turning the bag occasionally to coat the chops completely. Grill as desired. Serves 6.

Grill the chops over medium-hot coals for 2 minutes. Turn and grill for 1 minute. Scatter the coals to reduce the heat of the barbecue and grill the chops for 4 minutes. Turn and grill for 4 to 6 minutes, or cooked according to your preference.

Preheat the grill for 10 to 15 minutes on high heat. Turn off 1 burner and turn the remaining burner(s) to medium. Place the chops on the burner that is off and grill for 15 to 20 minutes, or according to your preference.

Preheat the contact grill to medium-high heat. Grill the chops for 5–6 minutes, or until cooked as desired.

Smokin' Hot Rubbed Pork Loin Chops

A rub with personality gives these chops everything needed for an outstanding entrée!

◆ ◆ ◆

1/2 cup dark brown sugar, packed

1/4 teaspoon cayenne pepper

1/4 teaspoon ground cinnamon

1/2 teaspoon California-style garlic salt

1 tablespoon freshly ground black pepper

1 tablespoon chili powder

1 tablespoon ground paprika

6 boneless pork loin chops, cut 1 to 1 1/2 inches thick

◆ ◆ ◆

Combine the sugar, pepper, cinnamon, garlic salt, pepper, chili powder and paprika. Mix thoroughly in a small bowl until all spices are well-incorporated. Place the chops in a large glass baking pan and generously dust with the rub. Press the rub into each chop. Turn the chops and dust each chop again with rub. Press the rub into each chop. Cover tightly with plastic wrap and refrigerate for 1 hour or up to 12 hours. Grill as directed. Serves 6.

C Grill over medium coals for 3 minutes. Turn and grill for 3 minutes. Move the coals away from direct heat and continue grilling the chops for 8 to 12 minutes on each side, or until cooked to your preference.

G Preheat the grill for 10 to 15 minutes on high heat. Turn off 1 burner and turn the remaining burner(s) to medium. Place the chops on the burner that is off and grill for 13 to 20 minutes, or according to your preference.

I Preheat the contact grill for 5 minutes on medium heat. Grill for 5 minutes. Turn the chops and grill for 4–5 minutes, or until cooked to your preference.

Tender Greek Pork Kebobs

Coriander and lemon bring the essence of
Greece to these kebobs.

◆ ◆ ◆

1/4 cup fresh lemon juice

1/2 cup extra virgin olive oil

2 tablespoons onion, finely minced

2 cloves garlic, finely minced

1 teaspoon ground coriander

1/2 teaspoon ground cumin

1/2 teaspoon cayenne pepper

1/8 teaspoon ground ginger

1/8 teaspoon ground allspice

2 pounds boneless pork, cut into 1-inch
   cubes

8 metal or bamboo skewers

◆ ◆ ◆

Prepare the marinade by combining the lemon juice, oil, onion, garlic, coriander, cumin, pepper, ginger and allspice. Mix well and pour into a large, self-sealing plastic bag. Add the pork cubes and mix well. Refrigerate for 2 hours or up to 12 hours. Place the pork on each of the 8 metal skewers evenly. If using bamboo skewers, soak the skewers in water for 10 minutes, drain and pat dry. Thread the pork onto the bamboo skewers while the skewers are still damp. Grill as directed. Serves 6–8.

C Grill the kebobs over medium coals for 5 minutes. Turn and baste the kebobs with the marinade. Grill for 5 minutes. Turn and grill the kebobs for 3–4 minutes, basting occasionally until cooked to your preference.

G Preheat the grill for 10 to 15 minutes on high heat. Turn 1 burner off and turn the remaining burner(s) to medium. Place the kebobs over the burner that is off. Close the lid and grill for 10 to 15 minutes, turning the skewers once.

 Preheat the contact grill for 5 minutes. Grill the kebobs for 6 minutes. Turn the kebobs and grill for 4 minutes, or until cooked to your preference.

Mediterranean Lamb Burgers

*Tuck these remarkable burgers into
whole wheat pita rounds.*

◆ ◆ ◆

2 pounds ground lamb

1/2 cup sweet onion, minced

4 cloves garlic, minced

1/4 cup fresh cilantro, minced

1/2 teaspoon ground cinnamon

1/2 teaspoon ground paprika

1/2 teaspoon ground cumin

1/2 teaspoon ground coriander

1/2 teaspoon chili powder

3 whole wheat pita rounds, cut in half

3 cups romaine lettuce, shredded

1/4 cup sour cream

6 slices sweet purple onion

6 slices ripe tomato

◆ ◆ ◆

Place the lamb in a large mixing bowl and lightly toss with your fingertips. Add the onion, garlic, cilantro, cinnamon, paprika, cumin, coriander and chili powder. Toss lightly to combine thoroughly. Do not overmix or the meat will become tough. Shape into 6 equal patties and grill as directed. Place 1 grilled lamb burger in each pita half and arrange the lettuce, sour cream, onion and tomato evenly over each burger. Serves 6.

Grill the lamb over medium coals for 5 minutes. Turn and grill for 4–6 minutes, or until cooked to your preference. Do not handle the meat more than is necessary.

Preheat the grill for 15 minutes on high heat. Turn all burners to medium and grill the burgers for 4 to 5 minutes on each side, or until cooked as desired. Turn the burgers once while grilling. Do not handle the meat more than is necessary.

Preheat the contact grill for 5 minutes. Cook for 5 minutes or until grilled as desired.

Moroccan Lamb Shish Kebobs

❖ ❖ ❖

1 1/2 to 2 pounds boneless lamb, cut into
    1-inch cubes

1/4 cup soy sauce

1/2 cup vegetable oil

2 green onions, minced

2 cloves garlic, minced

1 teaspoon ground ginger

1/4 cup honey

8 long metal or bamboo skewers

8 crimini mushrooms, cleaned and cut in
    half

1 orange bell pepper, cut into large squares

1 white onion, cut into large squares

❖ ❖ ❖

Place the lamb in a large, self-sealing plastic bag. Add the soy sauce, oil, green onions, garlic, ginger and honey and refrigerate for 4 hours. If using bamboo skewers, soak each in water for 10 minutes. Remove and drain the skewers. Thread the vegetables with the lamb on each skewer, alternating the vegetables and the meat. Grill as directed. Serves 4.

C Grill the kebobs over medium-hot coals for 2 minutes. Turn and grill for 2 minutes to seal in the juices. Cover and grill for 14 to 15 minutes or until the lamb is cooked as desired.

G Preheat the grill for 10 to 15 minutes on high heat. Reduce the heat to medium, place the skewers on the grill and cook for about 15 to 20 minutes, turning once or twice.

I Preheat the contact grill for 5 minutes. Place the kebobs in the grill and cook for 8–10 minutes, turning if necessary to grill all sides.

◆◆◆

Garlic & Rosemary Butterflied Leg of Lamb

Garlic and rosemary are the quintessential favorites for lamb of any cut. This butterflied leg of lamb grills into a tender and very flavorful entrée.

◆ ◆ ◆

4 to 6 pounds leg of lamb, boned, trimmed and butterflied

6 cloves garlic, cut into very thin slices

1 tablespoon dried rosemary, crushed

1 teaspoon salt

1 teaspoon freshly ground black pepper

◆ ◆ ◆

◆◆◆

Place the lamb on a large working surface. With the tip of a very sharp knife, make several small slits over the entire leg of lamb. Insert the slices of garlic into the small pockets. Sprinkle the rosemary into the leg of lamb, pressing slightly with your fingertips. Sprinkle the salt and pepper over the leg of lamb. Grill as directed. Serves 6–8.

C Grill over medium-hot coals for 2 minutes. Turn and grill for 2 minutes to completely sear the meat. Cover and grill for about 1½ hours. Use a meat thermometer to register the temperature at 160°F for medium-well, or until cooked to your preference. Allow the lamb to stand for 5–10 minutes prior to carving.

G Preheat the grill for 10 to 15 minutes on high heat. Grill the lamb for 5 minutes on high heat, turn and grill for 5 minutes. Reduce the heat to medium. Close the lid and grill for about 2 hours. Use a meat thermometer to register the temperature at 160°F for medium-well. Remove the lamb from the grill and let stand for 5 to 10 minutes prior to carving.

❖❖❖❖❖❖❖❖❖❖❖❖❖❖❖❖❖❖❖❖❖❖❖❖❖❖❖❖❖❖❖❖❖❖❖❖❖❖❖

Red Pepper-Rubbed Lamb Chops

*Lamb chops are delicious when grilled with
just a touch of garlic salt and pepper. However,
you can also dress up the chops for a special
dinner party by including this spicy rub.*

❖ ❖ ❖

12 lamb rib chops (about 4 ounces each)

2 tablespoons dark brown sugar

2 teaspoons crushed red pepper

1/2 teaspoon ground cumin

1 teaspoon garlic powder

1 teaspoon freshly ground black pepper

❖ ❖ ❖

Place the lamb chops on a flat surface. Combine the remaining ingredients in a small bowl. With your fingertips, lightly press the rub into each chop, covering as much of each chop as possible on both sides with the rub. Grill as directed. Serves 4.

 Grill over medium-hot coals for 3 minutes. Turn and grill for 5 to 8 minutes, or until cooked as desired.

Preheat the grill for 10 to 15 minutes on high heat. Turn off 1 burner and reduce the remaining burner(s) to medium. Place the chops on the grill and cook for 10 to 15 minutes. Turn once while grilling.

 Preheat the contact grill for 5 minutes. Grill the chops for 4 to 6 minutes, or until the chops are browned and cooked as desired.

Dark & Sweet Molasses Lamb

*A sweet and rich molasses glaze
enhances these chops.*

◆ ◆ ◆

1 cup dark molasses

2 teaspoons dry mustard

2 tablespoons apple cider vinegar

3 cloves garlic, minced

6 lamb loin chops

❖❖❖❖❖❖❖❖❖❖❖❖❖❖❖❖❖❖❖❖❖❖❖❖❖❖❖❖❖❖❖❖❖❖❖❖

Mix together in a small bowl the molasses, mustard, vinegar and garlic. Grill the chops as directed. Serves 6.

C Place the chops on the grill over medium-hot coals. Liberally brush with the sauce. Grill for 5 minutes and turn the chops. Brush with the sauce again and grill for 3 minutes. Turn again, brush the chops with sauce and grill for 2 minutes. Turn the chops for the last time, brush with sauce and grill for 2 minutes.

G Preheat the grill for 10 to 15 minutes on high heat. Reduce the heat on each burner to medium and place the chops on the grill. Brush with the sauce and grill for 5 minutes. Turn and brush with the sauce again. Grill for 5 to 7 minutes, turning once.

I Preheat the contact grill for 5 minutes. Place the chops in the grill and brush with the sauce. Grill for 3 minutes and brush with additional sauce. Grill for 2 minutes and brush with the sauce again. Check the chops for doneness and continue grilling, if needed, brushing the sauce over the chops as they cook.

❖❖❖❖❖❖❖❖❖❖❖❖❖❖❖❖❖❖❖❖❖❖❖❖❖❖❖❖❖❖❖❖❖❖❖❖

CHAPTER FIVE

SENSATIONAL GRILLED POULTRY!

Lime Chicken Satay with Warm Peanut Sauce

Garlicky Lime Basted Chicken Thighs

Zingy Hot BBQ Chicken Wings

Lemon & Fresh Herb Chicken Breasts

Sicilian Grilled Chicken & Garlic

MaryAnn's Polynesian Glazed Chicken

Caribbean Jerk Chicken Skewers

Poblano Grilled Chicken Quesadillas

White Wine & Lemon Herb Chicken

Super BBQ Chicken with Horseradish Sauce

Pineapple & Lime Grilled Tropical Chicken

Sweet Down South Barbecue Chicken

Buffalo Bill's Grilled Chicken

Turkey Medallions in Ginger-Orange Marinade

Turkey Breast a la Fiesta

❖❖❖❖❖❖❖❖❖❖❖❖❖❖❖❖❖❖❖❖❖❖❖❖❖❖❖❖❖❖❖❖

Introduction

C hicken and turkey are natural partners for the grill. Poultry adapts wonderfully to marinades, sauces and rubs and the juices from the poultry are retained because of the searing heat of the grill. Even the simplest chicken drumsticks grilled with bottled barbecue sauce will please the pickiest of eaters, simply because the smoked flavors imbue the chicken with the most delightful taste.

Poultry can be tricky on the grill. USDA guidelines recommend that poultry be grilled until it is completely cooked through at temperatures of 160°F to 170°F for food safety reasons. Boneless breasts can be tested quickly and grill most uniformly. If you are grilling poultry that is bone-in, don't be in a hurry to get the job done.

Give your grilled bone-in poultry the minimum suggested time and plan on additional time to cook your poultry to perfection. There should be no pink left in the meat of the poultry when you are ready to serve the food. Use medium coals or burners and close the lid of your grill so that the food cooks more evenly. Try to avoid turning the poultry over and over, as this causes drying. Baste the poultry, if possible, from time to time and allow the grill to do the work.

Inside this chapter you'll find creative recipes that start on a familiar note and build from there, you'll find many wonderful marinades and sauces to accompany your poultry and you'll delight in the specialty recipes perfect for guests or large crowds.

❖❖❖❖❖❖❖❖❖❖❖❖❖❖❖❖❖❖❖❖❖❖❖❖❖❖❖❖❖❖❖❖

◆◆◆◆◆◆◆◆◆◆◆◆◆◆◆◆◆◆◆◆◆◆◆◆◆◆◆◆◆◆◆◆◆◆◆◆◆◆

Lime Chicken Satay with Warm Peanut Sauce

Incorporate this chicken into an appetizer course or serve as an entrée for guests—either way it's sure to please!

◆ ◆ ◆

6 boneless, skinless chicken breast halves, cut into strips 3 inches long by 1/2-inch wide

2 tablespoons dark brown sugar

2 teaspoons curry powder

2 tablespoons creamy peanut butter

1/2 cup soy sauce

1/2 cup lime juice

3 cloves garlic, minced

pinch chili powder

20 short bamboo skewers

Warm Peanut Sauce

1 cup creamy peanut butter

1/2 cup coconut milk

2 tablespoons lime juice

2 tablespoons soy sauce

1 teaspoon ground ginger

2 cloves garlic, minced

◆ ◆ ◆

◆◆◆◆◆◆◆◆◆◆◆◆◆◆◆◆◆◆◆◆◆◆◆◆◆◆◆◆◆◆◆◆◆◆◆◆◆◆

Place the chicken breasts in a large, self-sealing plastic bag. Add the brown sugar, curry powder, peanut butter, soy sauce, lime juice, garlic and chili powder. Mix together thoroughly and refrigerate for 4 to 6 hours. Soak the bamboo skewers in water for 10 minutes, drain and pat dry. Remove the chicken from the marinade and thread the chicken onto the bamboo skewers. Grill as directed. Serve with the *Warm Peanut Sauce* at the table. Serves 6.

To prepare the *Warm Peanut Sauce*, combine in a small saucepan the ingredients as listed. Stir and mix over low heat until the peanut butter is blended into the sauce and the sauce is steaming. Remove from the heat and serve while warm at the table with the grilled chicken.

Grill the chicken skewers over hot coals for 3 minutes. Turn and grill for 6 to 7 minutes, or until cooked through.

Preheat the grill for 10 to 15 minutes on high heat. Reduce the heat to medium and grill the chicken skewers for 10 to 12 minutes, or until cooked through.

Preheat the grill for 5 minutes. Add the chicken skewers and grill for 4–5 minutes, or until cooked through.

Garlicky Lime Basted Chicken Thighs

This very zesty marinade dresses up the moist chicken thighs with élan!

◆ ◆ ◆

1/2 cup fresh lime juice

3 cloves garlic, finely minced

1/4 cup vegetable oil

2 tablespoons fresh cilantro, chopped

2 green onions, thinly sliced

1 teaspoon ground ginger

2 teaspoons chili powder

8 boneless, skinless chicken thighs

◆ ◆ ◆

Mix together the lime juice, garlic, oil, cilantro, onions, ginger and chili powder in a large, self-sealing plastic bag. Add the chicken thighs and refrigerate for 4 to 6 hours. Grill as directed. Serves 4.

Grill the chicken thighs over medium coals for 6 minutes. Turn and baste with the marinade. Grill for 6 to 8 minutes, or until completely cooked through.

Preheat the grill for 10 to 15 minutes on high heat. Reduce the heat to medium and add the thighs. Close the lid and grill for 15 to 18 minutes, or until cooked completely through. Baste occasionally while grilling.

Preheat the contact grill for 5 minutes. Grill the thighs for 6 to 8 minutes, or until cooked completely through.

Zingy Hot BBQ Chicken Wings

*Have cold drinks at hand to put out the fire
after sampling these fun appetizers!*

◆ ◆ ◆

2 pounds chicken wings

1/2 cup soy sauce

2 tablespoons hoisin sauce

2 tablespoons chili sauce

1/4 cup honey

1/4 cup vinegar

3 cloves garlic, minced

1/2 teaspoon chili powder

1/2 teaspoon freshly ground black pepper

◆ ◆ ◆

Place the chicken wings in a large glass pan. Mix together the remaining ingredients and cover the wings evenly. Wrap tightly with plastic wrap and refrigerate for 2 hours or up to 6 hours. Grill as directed. Serves 6 as an appetizer.

C Grill the wings over medium coals for 6 minutes. Turn and close the grill. Grill for 20 minutes, or until cooked completely through.

G Preheat the grill on high heat for 10 to 15 minutes. Reduce the heat to medium and grill the wings for 20 to 25 minutes, or until cooked through completely.

Lemon & Fresh Herb Chicken Breasts

Grilled chicken with light accompaniments—
perfect for a hot summer day!

◆ ◆ ◆

8 boneless, skinless chicken breasts

1/2 cup fresh lemon juice

4 cloves garlic, minced

1/4 cup vegetable oil

2 teaspoons fresh tarragon, minced

2 teaspoons fresh marjoram, minced

1 teaspoon freshly ground black pepper

1 teaspoon salt

◆ ◆ ◆

Place the chicken breasts in a large glass pan. Mix together the remaining ingredients and pour over the chicken. Cover tightly with plastic wrap and refrigerate for 4 to 6 hours. Turn the chicken breasts once or twice. Grill as directed. Serves 8.

Grill the chicken over medium coals for 6 minutes. Turn and baste with the marinade. Continue grilling for 4 to 6 minutes, or until the chicken is cooked through completely.

Preheat the grill for 10 to 15 minutes on high heat. Reduce the heat to medium and grill the chicken for 12 to 14 minutes, basting often, until cooked through completely.

Preheat the contact grill for 5 minutes. Grill the chicken for 5 to 6 minutes, basting once or twice, until cooked through completely.

Caribbean Jerk Chicken Skewers

Sweet and tangy meets hot and spicy!

❖ ❖ ❖

1 cup vegetable oil

4 cloves garlic, roughly chopped

1 large purple onion, roughly chopped

2 habañero peppers, seeded and chopped

2 tablespoons fresh parsley, chopped

1/4 cup cider vinegar

1/4 cup dark brown sugar, packed

1/4 teaspoon ground cinnamon

1/8 teaspoon ground cloves

1 1/2 teaspoons ground allspice

1/4 cup fresh lime juice

2 pounds boneless, skinless chicken breasts, cut into 1-inch cubes

12 long bamboo or metal skewers

❖ ❖ ❖

Combine all of the ingredients except the chicken and process in a blender for 2 minutes, or until smooth. Place the chicken in a glass pan and pour the sauce over the chicken. Marinate in the refrigerator for at least 2 hours or up to 6 hours. If using bamboo skewers, soak them in water for 10 minutes. Remove and drain. Grill as directed. Serves 6.

Grill the chicken over medium coals for 8 minutes. Turn and grill for 5-8 minutes, or until the chicken is completely cooked through.

Preheat the grill for 10 to 15 minutes on high heat. Reduce the heat to medium and grill the skewers for 8 minutes. Turn the chicken, close the lid and grill for another 8 to 10 minutes, or until the chicken is cooked through completely.

Preheat the contact grill for 5 minutes. Add the skewers and grill the chicken for 8 minutes. Check for doneness and continue cooking, if necessary until the meat is cooked through completely.

Poblano Grilled Chicken Quesadillas

Poblano chilies add a snap of extra flavor to these delicious grilled quesadillas.

◆ ◆ ◆

3 boneless, skinless chicken breast halves

1/2 teaspoon garlic powder

1/2 teaspoon ground chili powder

1/2 teaspoon poblano chilies, finely minced

1/2 teaspoon freshly ground black pepper

4 large whole wheat soft tortillas

1 1/2 cups pepper Jack cheese, shredded

1/4 cup sour cream

2 green onions, minced

◆ ◆ ◆

Place the chicken breasts on a flat surface. Mix together the garlic powder, chili powder, chilies and pepper and press the mixture into the chicken breasts on all sides. Grill as directed. Chop the grilled chicken in small pieces.

To serve, place 1 tortilla on a work surface and cover one-half with the cheese. Place several small dollops of sour cream on the cheese. Arrange the chicken on top and scatter the green onions over all. Fold the quesadillas in half and brush with oil if desired. Grill for 2 to 3 minutes, or until the cheese is softened and the tortilla is warm. Cut each tortilla into wedges and serve immediately with guacamole and/or salsa. Serves 4.

C Grill the chicken over medium coals for 6 minutes. Turn and continue grilling for 4 to 6 minutes, or until the chicken is cooked through completely.

G Preheat the grill for 10 to 15 minutes on high heat. Reduce the heat to medium and grill the chicken for 12 to 14 minutes, or until cooked through completely.

I Preheat the contact grill for 5 minutes. Grill the chicken for 5 to 6 minutes, or until cooked through completely.

◆◆◆

Pineapple & Lime Grilled Tropical Chicken

*Fresh juices bring a tropical appeal
to this tender grilled chicken.*

◆ ◆ ◆

2 cups fresh or frozen, reconstituted
   pineapple juice

1/4 cup fresh lime juice

1/4 cup soy sauce

1/4 cup vegetable oil

1/4 cup honey

3 cloves garlic, minced

1 teaspoon salt

1/2 teaspoon freshly ground black pepper

2 teaspoons fresh cilantro, minced

3 to 4 pounds roasting chicken, cut into
   serving pieces

◆ ◆ ◆

◆◆◆

❖❖❖❖❖❖❖❖❖❖❖❖❖❖❖❖❖❖❖❖❖❖❖❖❖❖❖❖❖❖❖❖❖❖❖❖

Mix together in a large bowl the pineapple juice, lime juice, soy sauce, oil, honey, garlic, salt, pepper and cilantro. Place the chicken in a large glass baking pan and pour the marinade over the chicken. Refrigerate for 2 or up to 6 hours. Grill the chicken as directed, basting often with the marinade. Serves 4.

C Grill the chicken over medium coals for 15 to 25 minutes, basting often with the marinade. Turn and grill for 20 to 30 minutes, or until the chicken is cooked through completely. Continue basting the chicken as it cooks.

G Preheat the grill for 15 minutes on high heat. Turn 1 burner off and reduce the heat on the remaining burner(s) to medium. Place the chicken, skin side up, over the burner that is off and close the lid. Grill the chicken for 45 minutes up to 1 hour, basting every 15 minutes with the marinade. Turn the chicken after about 30 minutes to brown both sides.

❖❖❖❖❖❖❖❖❖❖❖❖❖❖❖❖❖❖❖❖❖❖❖❖❖❖❖❖❖❖❖❖❖❖❖❖

Sweet Down South Barbecue Chicken

Most tomato-based barbecue sauces are tangy rather than sweet. In the South, both flavors are combined to make a memorable meal!

◆◆◆

1/4 cup Worcestershire sauce

1/4 cup butter, softened

1 cup ketchup

1/4 cup water

1 small white onion, chopped

2 cloves garlic, minced

2 tablespoons apple cider vinegar

3 tablespoons dark brown sugar

3 tablespoons molasses

2 teaspoons chili powder

1 teaspoon cayenne pepper

3 to 4 pounds roasting chicken, cut into serving pieces

◆◆◆

❖❖❖❖❖❖❖❖❖❖❖❖❖❖❖❖❖❖❖❖❖❖❖❖❖❖❖❖❖❖❖❖❖❖❖❖

Prepare the marinade by placing the Worcestershire sauce, butter and ketchup in a medium saucepan. Cook and stir over medium heat until the butter is melted and the ingredients are well-blended. Remove from the heat and add the water, onion, garlic, vinegar, sugar, molasses, chili powder and cayenne pepper. Mix again until well-combined.

Place the chicken in a large glass baking pan and pour the marinade over the chicken. Refrigerate for 2 or up to 6 hours. Grill the chicken as directed, basting often with the marinade. Serves 4.

Grill the chicken over medium coals for 15 to 25 minutes, basting often with the marinade. Turn and grill for 25 to 35 minutes, or until the chicken is cooked through completely. Continue basting the chicken as it cooks.

Preheat the grill for 15 minutes on high heat. Turn 1 burner off and reduce the heat on the remaining burner(s) to medium. Place the chicken, skin side up, over the burner that is off and close the lid. Grill the chicken for 45 minutes to 1 hour, basting every 15 minutes with the marinade. Turn the chicken after about 30 minutes to brown both sides.

❖❖❖❖❖❖❖❖❖❖❖❖❖❖❖❖❖❖❖❖❖❖❖❖❖❖❖❖❖❖❖❖❖❖❖❖

Turkey Medallions in Ginger-Orange Marinade

Turkey is a healthful entrée choice when eaten without the skin, however it can also become dry when overcooked. Watch the poultry carefully as it grills and test a few minutes before the recommended cooking time.

❖ ❖ ❖

6 boneless turkey medallions,
    about 3/4-inch thick

1 cup fresh orange juice

1/4 cup light molasses

2 teaspoons fresh ginger, finely grated

4 cloves garlic

1/4 cup vegetable oil

❖ ❖ ❖

Place the turkey in a large, self-sealing plastic bag. Add the remaining ingredients and combine well. Refrigerate for at least 1 hour or up to 4 hours. Grill as directed. Serves 6.

C Lightly oil the grids of the barbecue. Grill the turkey for 6 minutes over medium coals. Turn and grill for 8 to 9 minutes, or until cooked through completely.

G Lightly oil the grids before heating. Preheat the grill for 10 to 15 minutes on high heat. Reduce the heat to medium and add the medallions. Close the lid and grill for 6 to 7 minutes. Turn and grill for 7 to 11 minutes, or until cooked through completely.

I Preheat the contact grill for 5 minutes. Add the medallions and grill for 6 to 8 minutes, or until cooked through completely.

Turkey Breast a la Fiesta

Grilling a whole turkey breast requires a bit of attention and some extra time, however the results are well worth it, as this recipe proves!

◆ ◆ ◆

1 cup vegetable oil

1/4 cup orange juice

1/4 cup fresh lime juice

2 teaspoons chili powder

2 teaspoons dried sage leaves, crushed

1 teaspoon salt

1/2 teaspoon freshly ground black pepper

3 to 4 pounds boneless turkey breast

◆ ◆ ◆

Mix together in a medium bowl the oil, juices, chili powder, sage, salt and pepper. Place the turkey in a large glass pan and pour the marinade over the turkey. Cover tightly and refrigerate for 1 hour or up to 6 hours. Open the plastic wrap occasionally and turn the turkey breast as it marinates. Grill as directed. Serves 8.

C Grill the turkey breast, skin side down, over medium-hot coals for 6 to 8 minutes, or until the skin is golden and crisp. Turn and baste with some of the marinade. Arrange the coals slightly to reduce the heat and cover the turkey breast with aluminum foil. Grill for 30 to 40 minutes over medium coals or until the turkey is completely cooked through. Test with a meat thermometer. Let stand about 10 minutes before carving. Slice the turkey against the grain of the meat.

G Preheat the grill for 15 minutes on high heat. Place the turkey breast, skin side down, on the grill and cook for 8 minutes. Turn and baste with the marinade. Cover the turkey with foil and close the lid. Reduce the heat to medium and grill for 45 to 55 minutes and test with a meat thermometer. Let stand about 10 minutes before carving. Slice the turkey against the grain of the meat.

CHAPTER SIX

FRESH-FROM-THE-SEA GRILLED FISH!

Grilled Halibut with Tomato & Basil Coulee
Herb-Crusted Ahi Tuna Steaks
Outrageous Spice-Rubbed Salmon Fillets
Delicate Lemon Petrale Fillet of Sole
Marjoram-Dressed Swordfish Kebobs
Fresh Raspberry Grilled Sea Bass
Coconut Margarita Grilled Tilapia
Grilled Shark Steaks with Banana Mango Salsa
Grilled Red Snapper Veracruz
Salmon Steaks with Pineapple Teriyaki Glaze
Garlic-Drenched Grilled Shrimp Scampi
Buttery Grilled Scallop Kebobs

❖❖❖❖❖❖❖❖❖❖❖❖❖❖❖❖❖❖❖❖❖❖❖❖❖❖❖❖❖❖❖❖❖❖

Introduction

Many people shy away from grilling fish because of the thought that fish can be too delicate or difficult to handle on the grill. However, with proper tools, you'll find that the smoky essence of grilled fish is just about the best catch in the sea!

Try the recipes in this chapter that offer gourmet grilling—*Herb-Crusted Ahi Tuna Steaks, Marjoram-Dressed Swordfish Kebobs* and *Fresh Raspberry Grilled Sea Bass.* Or prepare a quick marinade or sauce for a simple evening meal, such as *Salmon Steaks with Pineapple Teriyaki Glaze, Garlic-Drenched Grilled Shrimp Scampi* or *Buttery Grilled Scallop Kebobs.* Either way, you'll soon look to your grill as the perfect partner when it comes to fish and shellfish!

Lightly oil the grids of your grill before grilling fish because fish will commonly stick to the grill. Fish is considered cooked when the fish flakes easily with a fork and is no longer opaque. For specialties such as Ahi tuna, you'll want to grill carefully according to the directions and use the freshest fish available.

Grilling baskets are a very handy tool when grilling fish. Oil the baskets or coat with cooking spray and place the fish or shellfish inside. You'll have the ability to grill your fish to the perfect finish without using a spatula or tongs or risking food falling through the grill.

❖❖❖❖❖❖❖❖❖❖❖❖❖❖❖❖❖❖❖❖❖❖❖❖❖❖❖❖❖❖❖❖❖❖

Grilled Halibut with Tomato & Basil Coulee

Halibut steaks are mild, but hold good consistency when grilled. This tomato coulee is a perfect foil to the mild fish.

◆ ◆ ◆

2 ounces fresh basil, cleaned and chopped

4 cloves garlic, chopped

1 tablespoon fresh lemon juice

8 ounce can tomato sauce

2 plum tomatoes, chopped

1 teaspoon freshly ground black pepper

1 teaspoon salt

2 tablespoons extra virgin olive oil

6 halibut steaks, about 1-inch thick

fresh basil for garnish

◆ ◆ ◆

Place the basil, garlic, lemon juice, tomato sauce, tomatoes, pepper, salt and oil in a food processor or blender. Pulse on medium for 2 minutes or until smooth. Remove and place in a small bowl. Grill the halibut steaks as directed. To serve, place a pool of the coulee on each individual plate and top with the halibut steaks. Garnish with additional basil leaves, if desired.

C Lightly oil the barbecue grids. Grill the halibut over medium coals for 3 minutes. Turn and continue grilling until the fish flakes easily and is cooked through.

G Lightly oil the barbecue grids. Preheat the grill for 10 to 15 minutes on high heat. Reduce the heat to medium and turn off 1 burner. Place the steaks over the burner that is off and close the lid. Grill for 6 to 7 minutes. Turn and continue grilling until the fish flakes easily and is cooked through.

I Coat the grill with cooking spray or oil. Preheat the grill for 5 minutes. Grill the steaks for 6 to 7 minutes, or until the fish flakes easily and is cooked through.

Herb-Crusted Ahi Tuna Steaks

*Purchase tuna steaks that are very,
very fresh and handle them carefully. This is
an entrée perfect for special guests.*

◆ ◆ ◆

**8 fresh Ahi tuna steaks, about 6 to 8
ounces each**

1/2 cup extra virgin olive oil

1/4 cup fresh cilantro, finely minced

1/4 cup fresh chervil, finely minced

2 tablespoons fresh parsley, finely minced

1 tablespoon lemon peel, finely minced

2 cloves garlic, minced

1 teaspoon salt

1 teaspoon freshly ground black pepper

◆ ◆ ◆

❖❖

Place the steaks on a flat surface. Process the oil, herbs, lemon peel, garlic, salt and pepper until smooth, about 2 minutes. Pat the herb mixture evenly onto 1 side of each steak. Grill as directed. Serves 8.

C Lightly oil the barbecue grids. Add the steaks and grill over medium coals for 4 minutes, herb side down. Turn and grill for 3 to 4 minutes for medium rare steaks, or as desired.

G Lightly oil the barbecue grids. Preheat the grill for 10 to 15 minutes on high heat. Reduce the heat to medium and grill the steaks for 4 minutes, herb side down. Turn and grill for 4 to 8 minutes for medium-rare steaks, or as desired.

I Coat the grill with cooking spray or oil. Preheat the grill for 5 minutes. Add the steaks and grill for 3 to 4 minutes for medium-rare steaks, or continue cooking as desired.

❖❖

Outrageous Spice-Rubbed Salmon Fillets

This rub has just about every spice in it!
Try it with all kinds of fish and poultry, too.

◆ ◆ ◆

1/4 teaspoon ground cloves

1/4 teaspoon ground allspice

1 teaspoon cayenne pepper

2 tablespoons ground paprika

1/2 teaspoon chili powder

1 teaspoon freshly ground black pepper

1 teaspoon garlic powder

2 teaspoons onion powder

2 teaspoons seasoned salt

2 tablespoons dark brown sugar

3 tablespoons granulated sugar

6 salmon fillets, 6 to 8 ounces each

◆ ◆ ◆

❖❖❖❖❖❖❖❖❖❖❖❖❖❖❖❖❖❖❖❖❖❖❖❖❖❖❖❖❖❖❖❖❖❖❖❖❖

Combine all of the ingredients except the salmon in a small bowl and rub with your fingertips to combine. Place the salmon fillets on a flat surface and gently rub and press the mixture into each fillet, covering as much of both sides of the fish as possible. Let stand for 5 minutes. Grill as directed. Serves 6.

C Lightly oil the barbecue grids. Grill the fish over medium coals for 5 minutes. Turn and grill for 5 to 8 minutes, or until the fish flakes easily.

G Oil the barbecue grids. Preheat the grill for 10 to 15 minutes on high heat. Turn off 1 burner and reduce the remaining burner(s) to medium heat. Place the fillets over the burner that is off and grill for 5 to 6 minutes. Turn and grill for 7 to 9 minutes, or until the fish flakes easily with a fork.

I Coat the grill with oil and preheat for 5 minutes. Add the fillets and grill for 6 to 8 minutes, or until the fish flakes easily with a fork.

❖❖❖❖❖❖❖❖❖❖❖❖❖❖❖❖❖❖❖❖❖❖❖❖❖❖❖❖❖❖❖❖❖❖❖❖❖

Delicate Lemon Petrale Fillet of Sole

Petrale fillet of sole is the champion of sole. The fillets are firm, yet tender and can hold up to grilling. This lemon and herb marinade is a delightful accompaniment to the fish.

◆ ◆ ◆

1/4 cup white vinegar

1 tablespoon fresh lemon juice

1/2 cup extra virgin olive oil

2 teaspoons salt

1 teaspoon garlic powder

1 teaspoon freshly ground black pepper

1 teaspoon dry mustard

4 petrale sole fillets, about 8 ounces each

lemon wedges for garnish

◆ ◆ ◆

Prepare the marinade by combining all of the ingredients except the sole fillets and lemon wedges. Place the fillets in a large glass pan and cover with the marinade. Wrap tightly and refrigerate for 1 hour or up to 2 hours. Turn once while marinating. Grill as directed. Serve with lemon wedges. Serves 4.

C Lightly oil the barbecue grids. Grill the fish over medium coals for 4 to 5 minutes. Turn and grill for 4 to 5 minutes, or until the fish flakes easily.

G Oil the barbecue grids. Preheat the grill for 10 to 15 minutes on high heat. Turn off 1 burner and reduce the remaining burner(s) to medium heat. Place the fillets over the burner that is off and grill for 4 to 5 minutes. Turn and grill for 4 to 5 minutes, or until the fish flakes easily with a fork.

I Coat the grill with oil and preheat for 5 minutes. Add the fillets and grill for 5 to 6 minutes, or until the fish flakes easily with a fork.

Marjoram-Dressed Swordfish Kebobs

Marjoram is a delightful herb that complements the texture of swordfish with ease. Grill the kebobs to medium-well for best results.

◆ ◆ ◆

1/4 cup fresh lemon juice

1/2 cup extra virgin olive oil

1 teaspoon dried marjoram

1 tablespoon lemon peel, grated

3 tablespoons ketchup

1 teaspoon salt

1 teaspoon freshly ground black pepper

1 clove garlic, finely minced

2 pounds swordfish fillets, cut into 1 1/2 inch cubes

8 bamboo or metal skewers

◆ ◆ ◆

Prepare the sauce by combining the lemon juice, olive oil, marjoram, lemon peel, ketchup, salt, pepper and garlic in a small bowl. If using bamboo skewers, soak them for 10 minutes in water and drain. Make the kebobs by threading the swordfish cubes on each skewer. Grill as directed. Serves 8.

 Lightly oil the barbecue grids. Grill the kebobs over medium coals for 6 to 8 minutes, brushing with the sauce once or twice. Turn the kebobs and brush with the sauce again. Grill for 6 to 7 minutes, or until cooked through.

Oil the barbecue grids and preheat the grill for 10 to 15 minutes on high heat. Turn off 1 burner and reduce the heat on the remaining burner(s) to medium. Grill the kebobs over the burner that is off for 7 to 9 minutes, brushing with the sauce occasionally. Turn and brush with the sauce again. Continue grilling for 7 to 8 minutes, or until cooked through.

Coat the grill with cooking spray. Brush the kebobs with the sauce. Grill the kebobs for 3 minutes and brush with the sauce again. Continue grilling for 4 to 6 minutes or until cooked through.

Fresh Raspberry Grilled Sea Bass

A twist on typical marinades, this lively raspberry marinade enhances the delicious grilled sea bass.

◆ ◆ ◆

1/4 cup fresh raspberries, washed and drained

1/4 cup fresh lemon juice

1/2 cup extra virgin olive oil

1/2 teaspoon dried Italian seasoning

1/2 teaspoon salt

1/2 teaspoon freshly ground black pepper

4 sea bass steaks, about 3/4-inch in thickness

◆ ◆ ◆

Place all of the ingredients except for the sea bass in a blender or food processor. Blend until completely combined, about 3 minutes. Place the steaks in a flat glass pan and cover with the raspberry marinade. Cover tightly and refrigerate for 1 hour. Grill as directed. Serves 4.

Lightly oil the barbecue grids. Add the steaks and grill over medium coals for 4 minutes. Turn and grill for 5 to 8 minutes, or until the fish flakes easily with a fork.

Lightly oil the barbecue grids. Preheat the grill for 10 to 15 minutes on high heat. Reduce the heat to medium and grill the steaks for 5 minutes. Turn and grill for 6 to 8 minutes, or until the fish flakes easily with a fork.

Coat the grill with cooking spray or oil. Preheat the grill for 5 minutes. Add the steaks and grill for 6 to 7 minutes, or until the fish flakes easily with a fork.

Coconut Margarita Grilled Tilapia

*Tilapia is a fish found in the warm
waters of the Pacific Ocean. You may substitute
mahi-mahi or any other mild fish if tilapia
is not available in your area.*

❖ ❖ ❖

1/4 cup Triple Sec

1/4 cup coconut milk

2 tablespoons gold tequila

1/4 teaspoon ground cinnamon

2 tablespoons dark brown sugar

2 tablespoons fresh lemon juice

1/2 teaspoon salt

1 1/2 to 2 pounds tilapia fillets

shredded coconut for garnish

❖ ❖ ❖

Mix together all of the ingredients except the tilapia. Place the fillets in a shallow glass pan and pour the marinade over the fish. Cover tightly and refrigerate for 1 hour. Grill as directed. Sprinkle the coconut evenly over the fillets to serve. Serves 4 to 6.

 Lightly oil the barbecue grids. Grill the fish over medium coals for 4 to 5 minutes. Turn and grill for 6 to 8 minutes, or until the fish flakes easily.

Oil the barbecue grids. Preheat the grill for 10 to 15 minutes on high heat. Turn off 1 burner and reduce the remaining burner(s) to medium heat. Place the fillets over the burner that is off and grill for 6 to 8 minutes. Turn and grill for 6 to 8 minutes, or until the fish flakes easily with a fork.

Coat the grill with oil and preheat for 5 minutes. Add the fillets and grill for 6 to 8 minutes, or until the fish flakes easily with a fork.

Grilled Shark Steaks with Banana Mango Salsa

A Jamaican delight—without leaving home!

◆ ◆ ◆

1/4 cup fresh lime juice

2 tablespoons fresh rosemary, crushed

1/4 cup extra virgin olive oil

2 tablespoons soy sauce

6 shark steaks, about 1-inch thick

Banana Mango Salsa

1 large banana, cut into small pieces

1 large mango, cut into small pieces

1/2 medium honeydew melon, cut into small chunks

1/2 cup purple onion, chopped

1 ripe tomato, cut into small pieces

1/4 cup fresh cilantro, finely minced

◆ ◆ ◆

To prepare the shark, combine the lime juice, rosemary, olive oil and soy sauce in a large, self-sealing plastic bag. Add the steaks and marinate for 1 hour. Grilled as directed and serve with the *Banana Mango Salsa*. Serves 6.

To prepare the *Banana Mango Salsa*, gently combine in a serving bowl, the banana, mango, melon, onion, tomato and cilantro. Allow the salsa to sit at room temperature for 1 hour prior to serving.

Lightly oil the barbecue grids. Grill the steaks over medium coals for 6 to 8 minutes, brushing with the marinade once or twice. Turn the steaks and brush with the marinade again. Grill for 6 minutes, or until cooked through completely.

Oil the barbecue grids and preheat the grill for 10 to 15 minutes on high heat. Turn off 1 burner and reduce the heat on the remaining burner(s) to medium. Grill the steaks over the burner that is off for 7 to 9 minutes, brushing with the marinade occasionally. Turn and brush with the marinade again. Continue grilling for 7 to 8 minutes, or until cooked through completely.

Coat the grill with cooking spray. Grill the steaks for 6 to 8 minutes or until cooked through completely.

Grilled Red Snapper Veracruz

*Veracruz, a charming port city in Mexico,
is famous for this grilled entrée.*

◆ ◆ ◆

4 red snapper fillets, about 8 ounces each

3 tablespoons vegetable oil

1 tablespoon ground paprika

1 teaspoon freshly ground black pepper

Veracruz Sauce

1/4 cup canned green chilies, chopped

1/4 cup pimento-stuffed green olives, sliced

1/4 cup extra virgin olive oil

1 small onion, chopped

4 small plum tomatoes, chopped

1 cloves garlic, minced

1/4 teaspoon ground cinnamon

1/4 teaspoon ground cloves

1/2 teaspoon brown sugar

2 tablespoons fresh lime juice

1 teaspoon salt

◆ ◆ ◆

❖❖❖❖❖❖❖❖❖❖❖❖❖❖❖❖❖❖❖❖❖❖❖❖❖❖❖❖❖❖❖❖❖❖❖❖

Place the red snapper fillets on a flat surface. Mix together the oil, paprika and pepper and smooth the mixture over both sides of each fillet. Grill as directed and serve with the *Veracruz Sauce*. Serves 4.

To prepare the *Veracruz Sauce,* sauté the green chilies and olives in the olive oil for 2 minutes over medium heat. Add the onion, tomatoes and garlic and sauté for 2 minutes. Add the cinnamon, cloves, brown sugar, lime juice and salt and blend well. Remove from the heat and spoon the sauce into a medium serving bowl. Top each grilled fillet with sauce and pass the remaining sauce at the table.

C Lightly oil the barbecue grids. Add the steaks and grill over medium coals for 5 minutes. Turn and grill for 5 to 8 minutes, or until the fish flakes easily with a fork.

G Lightly oil the barbecue grids. Preheat the grill for 10 to 15 minutes on high heat. Reduce the heat to medium and grill the steaks for 5 minutes. Turn and grill for 6 to 9 minutes, or until the fish flakes easily with a fork.

I Coat the grill with cooking spray or oil. Preheat the grill for 5 minutes. Add the steaks and grill for 5 to 8 minutes, or until the fish flakes easily with a fork.

❖❖❖❖❖❖❖❖❖❖❖❖❖❖❖❖❖❖❖❖❖❖❖❖❖❖❖❖❖❖❖❖❖❖❖❖

◆◆◆◆◆◆◆◆◆◆◆◆◆◆◆◆◆◆◆◆◆◆◆◆◆◆◆◆◆◆◆◆◆◆◆◆◆

Salmon Steaks with Pineapple Teriyaki Glaze

Look in the specialty food aisle of your grocery store for items such as Asian sesame oil and hoisin sauce.

◆ ◆ ◆

1 cup hickory-flavored barbecue sauce

2 tablespoons hoisin sauce

2 tablespoons Asian sesame oil

1 teaspoon prepared mustard

1 teaspoon ground ginger

2 cloves garlic, minced

2 tablespoons dark brown sugar

2 cups canned or fresh pineapple chunks

4 salmon steaks, about 1-inch thick

◆ ◆ ◆

◆◆◆◆◆◆◆◆◆◆◆◆◆◆◆◆◆◆◆◆◆◆◆◆◆◆◆◆◆◆◆◆◆◆◆◆◆

◆◆◆

Combine the barbecue sauce, hoisin sauce, sesame oil, mustard, ginger, garlic and sugar in a small saucepan. Stir and cook over low heat until well-blended. Remove from the heat and cool for 5 minutes. Grill the steaks as directed, brushing the steaks with the glaze. To serve, heat the remaining glaze again and add the pineapple chunks. Cook over low heat for 3 minutes. Cover each grilled steak with generous portions of the pineapple and glaze. Serves 4.

C Lightly oil the barbecue grids. Add the steaks and grill over medium coals for 6 minutes, brushing with the glaze once or twice. Turn and grill for 6 to 9 minutes, basting with the glaze again, until the salmon is cooked through completely.

G Lightly oil the barbecue grids. Preheat the grill for 10 to 15 minutes on high heat. Reduce the heat to medium and grill the steaks for 5 minutes. Brush the steaks with the glaze once or twice. Turn and brush the steaks with the glaze again. Grill for 6 to 10 minutes, basting occasionally, until the fish flakes easily with a fork.

I Coat the grill with cooking spray or oil. Preheat the grill for 5 minutes. Add the steaks and brush each with the glaze. Grill for 2 minutes. Brush again with the glaze. Grill for 5 to 7 minutes, or until the fish flakes easily with a fork.

◆◆◆

Garlic-Drenched Grilled Shrimp Scampi

If you like the taste and essence of garlic, this recipe is for you! Shrimp takes only a few moments on the grill so watch carefully while grilling.

❖ ❖ ❖

20 raw jumbo shrimp, shelled, deveined and rinsed

3/4 cup dry white wine

1/4 cup vegetable oil

4 cloves garlic, finely minced

1/2 teaspoon white pepper

1/4 teaspoon crushed red chilies

1 tablespoon fresh cilantro, chopped

❖ ❖ ❖

Place the shrimp in a large, self-sealing plastic bag and add the remaining ingredients. Marinate in the refrigerator for 1 hour. Grill as directed. Serves 4.

C Lightly coat a seafood barbecue tray with oil. Discard the marinade and place the shrimp on the tray and grill over medium coals for 3 minutes. Turn once and grill for 2 to 3 minutes, or until the shrimp turn uniformly opaque.

G Lightly coat a seafood barbecue tray with oil. Preheat the grill for 10 to 15 minutes on high heat. Discard the marinade and place the shrimp on the tray. Reduce the heat to medium and grill the shrimp for 3 minutes. Turn once and grill for 2 to 4 minutes, or until the shrimp turn uniformly opaque.

I Preheat the contact grill for 5 minutes. Discard the marinade. Place the shrimp in the grill and cook for 4 to 5 minutes, or until the shrimp turn uniformly pink.

❖❖❖❖❖❖❖❖❖❖❖❖❖❖❖❖❖❖❖❖❖❖❖❖❖❖❖❖❖❖❖❖

Introduction

If you think that your grill is for meat, poultry and seafood alone, stand back and get ready for some grilling adventures! Look through the pages of this chapter to find imaginative and simple recipes for side dishes, salads, vegetables and breads that either cook to a finish on the grill or accompany grilled foods to everyone's satisfaction.

When the days are warm and you'd like to stay out of the kitchen, opt for *Asian Steak Salad with Wild Greens* or *Pineapple & Toasted Sesame Seed Salad.* If you are entertaining and would like to set the tone of the evening with a spectacular beginning, use *Grilled Rosemary Polenta with Goat Cheese* or *Grilled Sweet & Tender Onions.* Even in the middle of winter, providing that your grill is located in an open, safe place for grilling, you'll enjoy *Grilled Rosemary Potatoes & Onions* and *Chile-Seasoned Grilled Corn.*

Homegrown vegetables are perfect when roasted and root vegetables take on a delightful, earthy sweetness when grilled. Experiment with your favorite vegetables and seasonings to see what works best for you. Whole vegetables, such as carrots and fennel, leeks and garlic, can be a delightful surprise. Vegetables with firm textures, such as eggplant and zucchini are perfect for the grill when sliced thickly, sprinkled with olive oil and balsamic vinegar and tossed onto the grill!

❖❖❖❖❖❖❖❖❖❖❖❖❖❖❖❖❖❖❖❖❖❖❖❖❖❖❖❖❖❖❖❖

Chile-Seasoned Grilled Corn

*Fresh ears of corn, basted with a
buttery chile sauce as they cook, are a
succulent side dish from the grill.*

◆ ◆ ◆

4 ears fresh corn on the cob, husks and silk
   removed

6 tablespoons butter, melted

1 clove garlic, minced

1/4 teaspoon crushed red chile pepper

1/2 teaspoon freshly ground black pepper

1 teaspoon salt

1 teaspoon fresh parsley, minced

◆ ◆ ◆

In a small bowl, whisk together the butter, garlic, red pepper, black pepper, salt and parsley. Grill as directed. Serves 4.

C Over moderately hot coals, place the corn on a grill that has been coated with cooking spray. Cover the grill and cook for 15 to 20 minutes, frequently turning the corn and brushing it with the butter sauce. The corn will be fork tender when ready to serve.

G Preheat the grill on medium-high heat for 10 minutes. Reduce the heat to medium. Place the corn evenly on the grill. Cover the grill and cook for 20 minutes, turning the corn frequently and basting with the butter sauce. The corn will be fork-tender when done.

I Preheat the contact grill for 5 minutes. Cut the cobs in half lengthwise, if needed, to fit in the grill. Space the corn evenly on the grill. Brush with the butter sauce, cover the corn and grill for 20 to 25 minutes. Baste with the sauce occasionally. The corn will be fork-tender when done.

Grilled Rosemary Potatoes & Onions

*Open these foil packages and the aroma
of potatoes, onions and herbs wafts upward.*

◆ ◆ ◆

4 large russet potatoes, cleaned

2 white onions, cut into wedges

4 tablespoons butter, cut into tablespoons

1 tablespoon fresh basil, minced

1 tablespoon fresh rosemary, minced

Salt and ground black pepper to taste

◆ ◆ ◆

Place each potato on a piece of foil big enough to wrap around the potato with room for sealing. Cut each potato into fourths *without* cutting through the potato completely. Evenly place the onions around and on top of the potatoes. Place one tablespoon of butter, cut into pieces, on each potato. Evenly sprinkle the herbs and the salt and pepper over each potato. Pull together the sides of the foil and seal each packet tightly. Wrap each potato in another square of foil. Grill as directed. Serves 4.

Over moderately hot coals, place the potatoes evenly on the grill. Cover the grill and cook the potatoes for 60 minutes. The potatoes will be done when they feel soft when squeezed gently. Remove the potatoes from the grill using barbecue mitts and remove the outer layer of foil. Serve the potatoes in the foil jackets on individual plates.

Preheat the grill on high heat for 10 to 15 minutes. Place the potatoes evenly on the grill. Reduce the heat to medium, cover the grill and cook for 1 hour and 15 minutes. Check the potatoes for doneness by gently squeezing each one. They will be soft when done. Remove the packets from the grill using barbecue mitts and remove the outer layer of foil. Serve the potatoes in the foil jackets on individual plates.

Grilled Navajo Bread

*Excellent when paired with grilled
chicken and salsa.*

❖ ❖ ❖

2 cups whole wheat flour

4 teaspoons baking powder

1 1/4 cups whole milk

1 egg

2 tablespoons vegetable oil

❖ ❖ ❖

In a large bowl, mix the flour and baking powder. Add the milk and egg and stir with a spoon until the bread batter is spongy. Prepare a cast iron skillet by placing the oil in the bottom and up the sides of the pan. Heat the oil in the skillet over the grill. Spoon the bread batter into the skillet. Grill the bread as directed. To serve, pull pieces of the bread and enjoy with grilled meats and/or beans. Serves 6.

C Place the skillet on the barbecue grill over medium-hot coals and cook for 15 minutes. When the bottom of the bread is brown, carefully turn the bread using 2 large spatulas. Grill again for about 15 minutes. Remove from the pan and cool slightly.

G Preheat the grill for 15 minutes on high heat. Reduce the heat to medium and place the bread in the skillet on the rack. Close the lid. Grill for 15 to 20 minutes. Turn the bread using 2 large spatulas and grill for an additional 15 minutes. Remove from the pan and cool slightly.

Art's Posole Chili

*Posole is a type of hominy commonly found
in Mexico. You may substitute canned hominy if
desired. Be sure to serve this chili with warmed
flour tortillas and grated cheese.*

◆ ◆ ◆

- 2 cups cooked posole
- 1/2 pound lean ground beef, cooked and crumbled
- 1/2 teaspoon liquid smoke
- 1 large yellow onion
- 2 cups canned pinto beans, drained
- 4 ripe tomatoes, chopped
- 15 ounce can tomato sauce
- 2 cloves garlic, minced
- 12 ounces Mexican beer

◆ ◆ ◆

Combine all of the ingredients in a slow cooker and stir
well to combine. Cook on Low for 6 to 8 hours or on
High for 3 to 4 hours. Stir occasionally. Serves 4.

Barbecued Whole Garlic

For an outstanding appetizer, try scooping the barbecued garlic onto warm slices of Italian bread.

◆ ◆ ◆

6 whole garlic bulbs
3 tablespoons extra virgin olive oil

◆ ◆ ◆

Lightly rub off any loose garlic skins. Cut the top of the bulbs off to expose each of the garlic heads inside. Sprinkle the cut side of each bulb with oil. Grill as directed. To serve, scoop the garlic from the bulbs and serve mounded on Italian bread or flatbread. Serves 12 as an appetizer.

C Grill the bulbs, cut side down, over medium coals for 20 minutes, or until the bulbs are very soft.

G Preheat the grill for 15 minutes on high heat. Reduce the heat to medium and turn off 1 burner. Place the bulbs over the burner that is off and close the lid. Grill for 20 to 30 minutes until the bulbs are very soft.

◆◆◆◆◆◆◆◆◆◆◆◆◆◆◆◆◆◆◆◆◆◆◆◆◆◆◆◆◆◆◆◆◆◆◆◆◆◆◆

Ginger Oil-Grilled Carrots

*Carrots develop a sweet, smoky
flavor when grilled—perfect for guests!*

◆ ◆ ◆

1/4 cup vegetable oil

1/2 teaspoon ground ginger

1/4 teaspoon salt

1 teaspoon fresh parsley, minced

6 large carrots, peeled and ends trimmed

◆ ◆ ◆

Blend the oil with the ginger, salt and parsley and set aside. Grill the carrots as directed, brushing with the ginger oil occasionally. To serve, cut the grilled carrots into slices about ½-inch in width and serve while warm. Serves 4 to 6.

C Grill the whole carrots over medium coals for 4 minutes, brushing with the oil occasionally. Turn and grill for 2 to 3 minutes, or until soft. Brush again with the oil.

G Preheat the grill for 10 to 15 minutes on high heat. Place the carrots on the grill and reduce the heat to medium. Brush with the oil and close the lid. Grill for 5 minutes. Turn the carrots and brush again with the oil. Grill for 3 to 4 minutes, or until the carrots are soft.

I Preheat the grill for 5 minutes. Cut the carrots in half lengthwise. Place the carrots in the grill and brush with the oil. Grill for 3 minutes. Brush again with the oil and continue grilling for 4 to 5 minutes, or until the carrots are soft.

Grilled Balsamic Vegetable Medley

*Add this robust mixture of vegetables
to a simple grilled chop or steak.*

◆ ◆ ◆

1 red pepper, cut into 1-inch squares

1 yellow pepper, cut into 1-inch squares

2 zucchini squash, washed and cut into
    1/4-inch thick slices

18 cherry tomatoes, washed

1 large purple onion, thickly sliced

18 crimini mushrooms, scrubbed and
    trimmed

1/2 cup extra virgin olive oil

2 tablespoons balsamic vinegar

1 teaspoon freshly ground black pepper

1/2 teaspoon salt

◆ ◆ ◆

Toss together the vegetables in a large glass or plastic bowl. Mix together the oil, vinegar, pepper and salt and pour over the vegetables. Turn and toss the vegetables again to coat. Refrigerate for 1 hour, turning the vegetables every 15 minutes. Grill as directed. Serves 4 to 6.

C Coat a perforated grilling tray with oil or cooking spray. Drain the vegetables from the oil and place in the tray. Grill over medium coals for 5 to 7 minutes, turning occasionally, until the vegetables are soft.

G Preheat the grill for 10 to 15 minutes on high heat. Reduce the heat to medium. Drain the vegetables from the oil and place the vegetables in a perforated grilling tray. Grill for 6 to 8 minutes with the lid closed, turning every 15 minutes until the vegetables are soft.

I Preheat the contact grill for 5 minutes. Drain the vegetables from the oil and place as evenly as possible in the grill, layering the vegetables if needed. Grill for 6 minutes, or until the vegetables are soft.

Grilled Italian Eggplant

Eggplant has a mild flavor that adapts well to the grill. The texture of this vegetable also partners well with Italian seasonings.

❖ ❖ ❖

1 large purple eggplant

2 tablespoons lemon juice

1/4 cup extra virgin olive oil

1 teaspoon dried Italian seasoning

1/2 teaspoon ground oregano

❖ ❖ ❖

Peel the eggplant and slice it into rounds about ½-inch thick. Combine the remaining ingredients in a small bowl. Grill as directed. Serves 4.

C Grill the eggplant slices over medium coals for 2 minutes. Brush with the oil and continue grilling for 2 minutes. Turn and brush with the oil again. Grill for 2 minutes and brush with the oil again. Grill for 2 minutes, or until the eggplant is browned and soft to the touch.

G Preheat the grill for 10 to 15 minutes on high heat. Reduce the heat to medium and place the eggplant slices on the grill. Brush with the oil and grill for 2 minutes. Brush with the oil again. Continue grilling for 2 minutes. Turn the eggplant and brush with the oil. Grill for 2 minutes. Brush again with the oil and grill until the eggplant is browned and soft to the touch.

I Preheat the contact grill for 5 minutes. Place the eggplant slices in the grill and brush with the oil. Grill for 4 minutes. Brush again with the oil. Continue grilling for 4 minutes or until the eggplant is browned and soft to the touch.

Easy Marinated Mushroom & Artichoke Skewers

◆ ◆ ◆

2 – 8 ounce jars marinated artichokes,
   oil reserved

3 cups small button mushrooms

10 bamboo or metal skewers

◆ ◆ ◆

Combine the artichokes and mushrooms with the oil in a large glass or plastic bowl. Cover tightly and refrigerate overnight. Turn the vegetables occasionally. If using bamboo skewers, soak the skewers for 10 minutes and drain. Thread the mushrooms and artichoke pieces onto the skewers, alternating each. Grill as directed. Serves 4 to 6.

C Grill the skewers over medium coals for 4 minutes. Turn and grill for 2 to 3 minutes or until the vegetables are browned and soft.

G Preheat the grill for 10 to 15 minutes on high heat. Reduce the heat to medium and grill the vegetables for 4 to 5 minutes. Turn and grill for 2 to 3 minutes or until the vegetables are browned and soft.

I Preheat the contact grill for 5 minutes. Grill the vegetables for 6 minutes or until the vegetables are browned and soft.

Whole Portobello Mushrooms with Soft Mozzarella Caps

Portobello mushrooms can easily be considered a main dish since the meat of the mushrooms is rich and filling. With the addition of the fresh mozzarella cheese, the grilled mushrooms are even more inviting!

◆ ◆ ◆

4 large portobello mushrooms, cleaned and dried

1/4 cup extra virgin olive oil

1 teaspoon freshly ground black pepper

1 teaspoon salt

1 tablespoon fresh lemon juice

4 slices fresh mozzarella cheese, about 1/8-inch thick

◆ ◆ ◆

◆◆◆◆◆◆◆◆◆◆◆◆◆◆◆◆◆◆◆◆◆◆◆◆◆◆◆◆◆◆◆◆◆◆◆◆◆◆◆

Place the mushrooms on a flat surface, stem side up. Sprinkle each with the oil, pepper, salt and lemon juice. Grill as directed. Serves 4.

C Grill the mushrooms over medium coals for 8 minutes, with the cut side down. Turn and place 1 slice of cheese over each mushroom. Grill for 3 minutes or until the cheese has softened over the mushrooms.

G Preheat the gas grill for 10 to 15 minutes on high heat. Reduce the heat to medium. Grill the mushrooms for 8 minutes, with the cut side down. Turn and place 1 slice of cheese over each mushroom. Grill for 3 minutes or until the cheese has softened over the mushrooms.

I Preheat the contact grill for 5 minutes. Place the mushrooms in the grill, cut side up. Grill for 6 to 8 minutes, or until the mushrooms are soft. Preheat the oven broiler. Remove the mushrooms from the grill and place 1 slice of mozzarella over each mushroom. Broil for 2 minutes, or until the cheese has softened over the mushrooms.

◆◆◆◆◆◆◆◆◆◆◆◆◆◆◆◆◆◆◆◆◆◆◆◆◆◆◆◆◆◆◆◆◆◆◆◆◆◆◆

◆◆◆

Grilled Sweet & Tender Onions

Vidalia onions take on a new personality when grilled. They become almost as sweet as candy!

◆ ◆ ◆

4 Vidalia onions, peeled and sliced
   1/4-inch thick

1/4 cup extra virgin olive oil

2 tablespoons fresh thyme, finely minced

1 teaspoon salt

1 teaspoon freshly ground black pepper

◆ ◆ ◆

◆◆◆

Place the whole slices on a flat surface. Sprinkle each with the olive oil, thyme, salt and pepper. Grill as directed. Serves 6 to 8.

C Grill the onion slices over medium coals for 3 minutes. Turn and grill for 2 to 3 minutes, or until soft.

G Preheat the grill for 10 to 15 minutes on high heat. Reduce the heat to medium and place the onion slices on the grill. Cook for 4 minutes. Turn and grill for 2 to 3 minutes or until soft.

I Preheat the contact grill for 5 minutes. Place the slices in the grill and cook for 5 minutes or until soft.

Grill-Roasted Potatoes

*While using a charcoal grill to prepare
your entrée, tuck these little packets of potatoes
directly on or near the briquets. The results are
crispy, tender and sweet-roasted potatoes.*

◆ ◆ ◆

**4 large baking potatoes, peeled and sliced
thinly**

1/4 cup white onion, chopped

1/4 cup butter, softened

1/2 teaspoon seasoned salt

1/4 teaspoon black pepper

◆ ◆ ◆

Prepare double-thicknesses of 4 large squares of foil.
Place equal portions of potatoes and onion in the center
of each square. Evenly divide the butter, seasoned salt
and pepper over the potatoes and close the foil packets
tightly. Grill the packets as directed. Serves 4 generously.

Grill directly in or next to medium coals. Shift and
turn the packets every 10 minutes or so, grilling
about 30 minutes total. The potatoes will be soft
and steaming when ready to serve. Remove the foil
carefully.

Creamy Parmesan Risotto

There is something deliciously soothing about this risotto, which makes it a perfect companion to any grilled meat, poultry or fish. Make sure you use arborio rice for best results.

❖ ❖ ❖

1 1/2 cups arborio rice

2 tablespoons extra virgin olive oil

1 purple onion, diced

1/2 cup button mushrooms, chopped

1 bay leaf

1 cup sweet white wine

41/2 cups chicken broth

1 cup Parmesan cheese, grated

1/4 cup fresh parsley, chopped

❖ ❖ ❖

Sauté the rice in the olive oil in a large pan for 2 minutes, stirring occasionally. Add the onion, mushrooms, bay leaf and wine. As the rice cooks add 4 cups of the chicken broth. Add a little more broth if all of the broth is absorbed before the rice is cooked tender, about 25 minutes. Check the rice periodically to determine whether or not the broth is absorbed and add a little broth at a time. When the rice is cooked, stir in the cheese and sprinkle with the parsley. Serves 6.

◆◆◆◆◆◆◆◆◆◆◆◆◆◆◆◆◆◆◆◆◆◆◆◆◆◆◆◆◆◆◆◆◆◆

Chopped Garden Vegetable Risotto

This risotto celebrates new vegetables in the early Spring. Enjoy it with grilled pork, lamb or poultry.

◆◆◆

1 white onion, chopped

2 tablespoons extra virgin olive oil

2 cups zucchini squash, finely diced

1 cup baby asparagus, chopped

1/2 cup carrots, diced

1 cup roma tomatoes, diced

1 teaspoon salt

1 teaspoon pepper

1 1/2 cups arborio rice

4 cups chicken broth, heated to almost boiling

1 cup dry white wine

1 tablespoon garlic flavored olive oil

◆◆◆

◆◆◆◆◆◆◆◆◆◆◆◆◆◆◆◆◆◆◆◆◆◆◆◆◆◆◆◆◆◆◆◆◆◆

Use a large saucepan to combine the onion and oil. Sauté the onion for 2 minutes until translucent. Add the squash, asparagus and carrots and cook and stir over low heat for 10 minutes. Add the tomatoes, salt and pepper and continue cooking for 15 minutes. Add the rice and a bit of the broth. Add the wine and stir. Continue cooking the rice and vegetables over low heat, adding broth every few minutes as the liquid is absorbed. Cook for about 20 to 30 minutes or until the rice is tender and fully cooked. Stir in the olive oil and serve. Serves 6.

Grilled Rosemary Polenta with Goat Cheese

Rosemary and goat cheese give this polenta superior flavor. Serve with grilled porterhouse steaks.

◆ ◆ ◆

8 cups chicken broth

2 cups finely ground yellow cornmeal

1/2 teaspoon salt

1/4 cup goat cheese, softened

2 tablespoons olive oil

1/2 teaspoon freshly ground black pepper

sprigs fresh rosemary, crumbled

◆ ◆ ◆

Butter the sides and bottom of a 9-inch by 13-inch baking dish. Heat the chicken broth in a large stockpot to a boil and slowly add the cornmeal. Whisk constantly after each small addition (this eliminates lumps in the polenta) until all of the cornmeal has been introduced to the broth. Reduce the heat to low and cook until thickened, about 15 minutes. Fold in the salt, goat cheese, oil and pepper and pour into the baking dish. Cover tightly with plastic wrap and refrigerate overnight. Cut the polenta into small squares and brush with olive oil and a few crumbles of the rosemary. Grill as directed. Serves 6 to 8.

Grill the polenta squares over medium coals for 2 minutes. Turn and continue grilling for 2 to 3 minutes, until golden brown.

Preheat the grill for 10 to 15 minutes on high heat. Reduce the heat to medium and grill the polenta squares for 3 minutes. Turn and grill for 3 minutes, or until golden brown.

Preheat the contact grill for 5 minutes. Grill the squares for 4 minutes or until golden brown.

Apricot & Walnut Wild Rice

An amazing array of tastes and textures steeped into a lovely wild rice. Serve with grilled poultry.

◆ ◆ ◆

1/2 cup celery, chopped

1 cup white onion, finely chopped

2 tablespoons extra virgin olive oil

12/3 cups wild rice

1 cup dry white wine

1 1/2 cups water

1 teaspoon fresh parsley, chopped

1/2 cup dried apricots, finely chopped

1/2 cup raisins, finely chopped

1/4 cup walnuts, finely chopped

1 teaspoon fresh sage, minced

◆ ◆ ◆

◆◆◆

Preheat the oven to 350°F. Lightly coat a 2 quart baking dish with cooking spray and set aside. Sauté the celery and onion in the oil in a medium saucepan for 2 minutes. Pour the vegetables into the baking dish and add the rice, wine, water, parsley, apricots, raisins, walnuts and sage. Mix well. Cover and bake for 1 hour, stirring every 15 minutes. If the rice is not tender after 1 hour, add a bit more water and continue cooking for 15 minutes. To serve, fluff the rice and garnish with additional walnuts, if desired. Serves 4.

◆◆◆

Spicy Baja Beans

Use a slow cooker to prepare these beans.
The time spent cooking only enhances
the zesty kick of the beans.

◆ ◆ ◆

2 cups navy beans

1 yellow onion, chopped

2 plum tomatoes, chopped

2 cloves garlic, minced

3 tablespoons dark molasses

1 teaspoon dry mustard

1/4 cup canned green chilies, chopped

1 teaspoon chili powder

◆ ◆ ◆

Soak the beans overnight in water to cover. Drain and cover the beans with fresh water in a large saucepan. Simmer the beans over low heat for 1 hour or until tender. Combine all of the remaining ingredients in a slow cooker and add the beans. Mix well. Cook on Low for 6 hours or on High for 3 to 4 hours. Serves 8.

Bootlegger's Cole Slaw

A little splash of whisky perks up this slaw! Serve alongside any hearty cut of grilled beef, chicken or pork.

◆ ◆ ◆

3 cups green cabbage, thinly sliced or grated

3 cups purple cabbage, thinly sliced or grated

2 medium carrots, peeled and grated

1/2 cup white onion, chopped finely

1 red pepper, diced

1/4 cup fresh parsley, minced

1 tablespoon Dijon mustard

1 tablespoon premium whiskey

1 cup prepared mayonnaise

2 tablespoons vegetable oil

1 teaspoon salt

1 teaspoon freshly ground black pepper

◆ ◆ ◆

Toss together the cabbage, carrots, onion, red pepper and parsley in a large serving bowl. Whisk together the remaining ingredients until smooth and pour over the vegetables. Toss again until well-blended. Refrigerate for 1 hour before serving. Serves 8.

◆◆◆◆◆◆◆◆◆◆◆◆◆◆◆◆◆◆◆◆◆◆◆◆◆◆◆◆◆◆◆◆◆◆◆◆◆◆

Asian Steak Salad with Wild Greens

Grilled flank steak is lean and tender when sliced thinly across the diagonal. Add the steak slices to a wonderfully Asian-dressed salad and you have an instant entrée for a warm summer evening!

◆◆◆

3/4 cup vegetable oil

1/4 cup soy sauce

2 cloves garlic, minced

3 green onions, chopped

1 teaspoon ground ginger

2 tablespoons clover honey

1 1/2 to 2 pounds flank steak

Asian-Dressed Salad

8 cups mixed wild greens

1 cucumber, peeled and chopped

1 carrot, peeled and cut into small matchstick pieces

1/4 cup peanut oil

1 tablespoon Asian sesame oil

1/2 teaspoon Asian chile oil

3 tablespoons rice wine vinegar

1/2 teaspoon sugar

1/2 cup thin crispy noodles

◆◆◆◆◆◆◆◆◆◆◆◆◆◆◆◆◆◆◆◆◆◆◆◆◆◆◆◆◆◆◆◆◆◆◆◆◆◆

To prepare the steak, combine the oil, soy sauce, garlic, green onions, ginger and honey in a large, self-sealing plastic bag. Add the flank steak and seal. Refrigerate for 6 hours. Grill as directed. Slice thinly across the diagonal and use the steak in the salad as directed. Serves 6.

To prepare the *Asian-Dressed Salad,* toss the greens in a very large salad bowl. Add the cucumber and carrots and toss again. Whisk together the oils, vinegar and sugar and pour over the greens and vegetables. Add the steak slices and toss again. Scatter the thin noodles over the top and serve immediately.

Grill the flank steak over medium coals for 20 to 25 minutes, or until cooked to medium-rare. Turn once while grilling and keep the lid closed for a lower heat.

Preheat the grill for 10 to 15 minutes on high heat. Reduce the heat to medium and place the steak on the grill. Close the lid and grill for 20 minutes. Turn and grill for 10 minutes, or until cooked to medium-rare.

Preheat the contact grill for 5 minutes. Place the steak in the grill and cook for 10 to 15 minutes, or until cooked to medium-rare.

Pineapple & Toasted Sesame Seed Salad

A simple salad to complement any grilled entrée. This is especially good with Asian grilled beef or chicken.

◆ ◆ ◆

2 tablespoons sesame seeds

2 tablespoons sesame seed oil

1/4 cup rice vinegar

1/2 cup pineapple juice

10 cups romaine lettuce, shredded

1/4 cup bean sprouts, cleaned and cut into 1-inch pieces

1 carrot, peeled and grated

1 cup canned mandarin orange segments, drained

◆ ◆ ◆

Pour the sesame seeds into a medium saucepan and cook over medium heat until browned and crispy. Stir constantly. Mix the seeds with the oil, vinegar and pineapple juice and whisk well. Combine the lettuce, bean sprouts, carrot and mandarin oranges in a large serving bowl. Pour the dressing over the salad and serve immediately.

Tri-Pepper Potato Salad

A sunny tribute to warm weather!

◆ ◆ ◆

2 pounds red potatoes, scrubbed and cut
   into cubes

1/4 cup purple onion, minced

1/2 red bell pepper, chopped

1/2 green bell pepper, chopped

1/2 yellow bell pepper, chopped

2 cloves garlic, minced

1/2 cup prepared mayonnaise

3 tablespoons fresh lime juice

1 teaspoon freshly ground black pepper

pinch chili powder

1/4 cup fresh cilantro, minced

◆ ◆ ◆

Steam the potatoes in a large stockpot until soft. Drain
and cool. In a large serving bowl, combine all of the
remaining ingredients and mix well. Add the potatoes
and combine again. Cover and refrigerate for at least 2
hours to allow the flavors to marry. Serves 6 to 8.

CHAPTER EIGHT

DELICIOUS GRILLED DESSERTS!

Puerto Rican Rum-Soaked Bananas

Golden Grilled Peaches with Crème Anglaise

Grilled Pineapple, Apple & Poundcake with
Hot Fudge Sauce

Grilled Lemon Pound Cake Fingers

Whole Pineapple in Maple & Grand Marnier™ Sauce

Date & Honey Relish with Ice Cream

Introduction

G rilled desserts are finding a new popularity among the most chic of restaurants. The most delicious and sweet fruits are made even better when grilled lightly with a touch of brown sugar and butter, so it's no wonder that patrons are lining up for restaurant grilled desserts.

Fruits adapt very well to the grill, so you'll find recipes in this chapter that feature cakes with fruit or fruit with ice cream or other dessert partners. If you've grilled an evening meal and are enjoying the last of the fire, try adding any fruit, light cake or bread to the grill –the results may surprise you!

Puerto Rican Rum-Soaked Bananas

Watch these bananas carefully to make sure they don't burn. The butter and rum bring out the best of the fruit.

❖ ❖ ❖

1/4 cup dark rum
1/4 cup dark brown sugar
3 tablespoons butter, softened
1/2 teaspoon ground cinnamon
6 small, firm bananas, peeled
dairy whipped cream

❖ ❖ ❖

Combine the rum, brown sugar, butter and cinnamon in a small bowl. Set aside. Cut each banana in half lengthwise and place on a perforated grilling tray. Arrange the banana halves, cut side up, on the tray. Lightly spread each banana with the rum and sugar mixture. Grill as directed. Top each banana with a dollop of whipping cream and serve while warm. Serves 6.

C Place the tray of bananas on the grill over medium coals. Close the lid and grill for 3 to 4 minutes, or until the rum and sugar sauce has melted and the bananas are warmed.

G Preheat the grill for 10 to 15 minutes on high heat. Reduce the heat to medium and place the tray of bananas on the grill. Close the lid and grill for 3 to 4 minutes, or until the rum and sugar sauce has melted and the bananas are warmed.

I Preheat the grill for 5 minutes. Do not use a grilling tray. Place the bananas directly in the grill and cook for 3 minutes, or until the rum and sugar sauce has melted and the bananas are warmed.

Golden Grilled Peaches with Crème Anglaise

A divine combination of sweet, grill-softened peaches and smooth sweet custard!

♦ ♦ ♦

2 tablespoons sugar

1/4 teaspoon vanilla extract

pinch salt

4 large egg yolks

1 cup whole milk

6 ripe peaches, peeled, halved and pitted

3 tablespoons unsalted butter softened

♦ ♦ ♦

❖❖❖❖❖❖❖❖❖❖❖❖❖❖❖❖❖❖❖❖❖❖❖❖❖❖❖❖❖❖❖❖❖❖

Combine the sugar, vanilla, salt and egg yolks in a small saucepan. Blend well until completely integrated. Scald the milk in another small saucepan. Cool slightly and sprinkle a few tablespoons of the milk into the egg yolk mixture. Whisk well. Slowly add the remaining milk, whisking constantly. Heat the custard to just below the boiling point, stirring constantly. The custard should be thickened and hot, but not boiling. Stir constantly and remove from the heat. Pour into 6 small custard dishes and cool at room temperature. Cover tightly and refrigerate until use. Grill the peaches as directed. To serve, top each cold custard with a warm grilled peach half. Serves 6.

C Grill the peach halves, cut side up for 3 minutes, brushing with butter occasionally. Turn and grill for 2 minutes, or until the peaches are soft. Serve immediately over the *Crème Anglaise*.

G Preheat the grill for 10 to 15 minutes on high heat. Reduce the heat to medium and place the peaches, cut side up on the grill. Grill for 3 minutes, brushing with the butter occasionally. Turn and grill for 2 to 3 minutes, or until the peaches are soft. Serve immediately over the *Crème Anglaise*.

I Preheat the contact grill for 5 minutes. Place the peaches, cut side up in the grill and brush with the butter. Grill for 3 to 4 minutes, or until the peaches are soft. Serve immediately over the *Crème Anglaise*.

❖❖❖❖❖❖❖❖❖❖❖❖❖❖❖❖❖❖❖❖❖❖❖❖❖❖❖❖❖❖❖❖❖❖

Grilled Pineapple, Apple & Poundcake with Hot Fudge Sauce

Grilling meets fondue in this fun recipe!

◆ ◆ ◆

2 cups fresh pineapple, cut into large chunks

2 tart green apples, peeled and cut into large chunks

1 loaf prepared pound cake, cut into 1 1/2-inch cubes

10 long metal skewers

Hot Fudge Sauce

3 ounces semisweet chocolate chips

1 tablespoons cocoa powder, unsweetened

1/4 cup water

2 tablespoons butter

1/4 cup sugar

2 tablespoons light corn syrup

pinch salt

1/2 teaspoon vanilla extract

◆ ◆

◆◆

Prepare the fruit and cake for the grill by alternately threading each onto the metal skewers. Set aside. Prepare the *Hot Fudge Sauce* by melting the chocolate chips, cocoa and water in a small saucepan over low heat. Stir occasionally. Add the butter, sugar, corn syrup and salt and simmer to dissolve the sugar. Raise the heat until the mixture comes to a boil and stir occasionally while boiling for 3 minutes. Reduce the heat to low and add the vanilla. Serve while warm. Grill the fruit as directed. To serve, remove the grilled fruit and cake from the skewers and drizzle each serving with the fudge sauce. Serves 5.

 Grill the fruit and cake kebobs over medium coals for 3 minutes. Turn and grill for 3 to 4 minutes, or until tender.

Preheat the grill for 10 to 15 minutes on high heat. Turn the burners to medium, place the fruit and cake skewers on the grill and cook for about 4 to 6 minutes, turning once or twice until the fruit is tender.

Preheat the contact grill to medium heat. Place the fruit and cake skewers evenly in the grill and cook for 5 minutes or until tender.

◆◆

Grilled Lemon Pound Cake Fingers

Grilled sweet cake with a cup of cream-laced coffee is a perfect conclusion to any meal.

◆ ◆ ◆

1 loaf frozen lemon pound cake, thawed
1/2 cup butter, softened
1/2 cup powdered sugar

◆ ◆ ◆

Cut the pound cake into fingers, about 3 inches in length and 2 inches in width. Dip each briefly in the butter on 1 side and then in the powdered sugar. Grill as directed. Serves 6 to 8.

C Grill the cakes over medium coals for 2 minutes. Turn and grill for 2 minutes or until lightly golden and toasted.

G Preheat the grill for 10 to 15 minutes on high heat. Turn the burners to medium, place the cakes on the grill and cook for about 2 minutes. Turn once and continue grilling until the cakes are lightly toasted and golden.

 Preheat the contact grill to medium heat. Place the cakes in the grill and cook for 3 minutes or until the cakes are lightly toasted and golden.

Whole Pineapple in Maple & Grand Marnier™ Sauce

Quite a luscious treat! Serve with
French vanilla ice cream, if desired.

❖ ❖ ❖

1 ripe, whole pineapple, quartered and sliced

1/2 cup premium maple syrup

1/2 teaspoon ground cinnamon

1 teaspoon Grand Marnier™

❖ ❖ ❖

Place the slices of pineapple back in the pineapple shells to make 4 servings. Combine the syrup, cinnamon and Grand Marnier in a small bowl. Set aside. Grill as directed, basting with the sauce. Serves 4.

C Grill the pineapple quarters, shell side down, over medium coals for 15 minutes. Baste with the sauce while grilling.

G Preheat the grill for 10 to 15 minutes on high heat. Turn the burners to medium, place the pineapples on the grill and cook for about 15 to 18 minutes. Baste with the sauce while cooking.

Date & Honey Relish with Ice Cream

◆ ◆ ◆

1/2 cup clover honey

1/4 cup fresh mint, minced

3 tablespoons lemon juice

2 cups dates, pits removed and chopped

1 teaspoon salt

1 quart premium vanilla ice cream

◆ ◆ ◆

Heat the honey in a nonstick pan over low heat until it begins to foam. Add the mint, lemon juice, dates and salt and stir well to combine. Remove from the heat and cool. Store in the refrigerator. To serve, pour the relish over any flavor of ice cream. Makes about 2 cups.

CHAPTER NINE

SUPREME SAUCES, SALSAS & MARINADES!

Kansas City-Style Barbeque Sauce

Ginger & Hot Pepper Sauce

Latin-American Rib Sauce

Smokey-the-Bear Sauce

Basil & Balsamic Vinegar Sauce

Orange Mustard Sauce

Pineapple Sweet & Sour Sauce

Cayenne Pepper Peanut Sauce

Maple Spice Sauce

Garlic Lemon Caper Sauce

Tangy Mustard Barbeque Sauce

Tomato & Chile Salsa

Jicama-Citrus Salsa

Tomatillo Salsa Verde

Pineapple Peach Salsa

MaryAnn's Garden Tomato Salsa

Texas Everything-Inside Salsa

Black Bean & Corn Salsa
Tropical Mango & Papaya Salsa
Red Onion Salsa
Teriyaki Mustard Marinade
Rum & Molasses Marinade
Delicate Herb Marinade
Island Marinade
Five-Spice Chinese Marinade
Spicy Onion Marinade
Southwestern Marinade
Snappy Fresh Citrus Marinade

❖❖❖❖❖❖❖❖❖❖❖❖❖❖❖❖❖❖❖❖❖❖❖❖❖❖❖❖❖❖❖❖❖❖❖❖

Introduction

Everyone has a "favorite, secret, special, handed-down-through-the-family" sauce or marinade that is a special pride and joy. My own family used one particular Asian-style marinade on grilled flank steak for almost every holiday of the year. It was special, it was unique and it was ours. We still pull it out when we gather for special meals, even though the family has tripled in size!

The sauces, salsas and marinades in this chapter will happily accompany your favorites or they will add originality to the bottled sauces and marinades available. If you are pressed for time, even the most basic oil-based salad dressing will qualify as a marinade. Try cheese-Italian or balsamic vinegar and oil. You will also find inspiration in your own combinations of seasonings and liquids. Use *Delicate Herb Marinade* as a starting place and build ingredients from there. An excellent sauce for almost everything is *Teriyaki Mustard Marinade* and you'll find the *Kansas City-Style Barbecue Sauce* marinade to adapt well to a wide variety of meats and poultry.

❖❖❖❖❖❖❖❖❖❖❖❖❖❖❖❖❖❖❖❖❖❖❖❖❖❖❖❖❖❖❖❖❖❖❖❖

Kansas City-Style Barbeque Sauce

*This is the familiar favorite style of
barbeque sauce. Make your own and enjoy
the freshness of traditional spices.*

◆ ◆ ◆

1/4 cup brown sugar, firmly packed

3 teaspoons chili powder

1/4 teaspoon cayenne pepper

1 teaspoon black pepper

2 teaspoons garlic powder

1/4 cup white vinegar

3 teaspoons Worcestershire sauce

1 cup ketchup

◆ ◆ ◆

In a nonreactive saucepan, combine the brown sugar, chili powder, cayenne pepper, black pepper and the garlic powder. Blend in the vinegar and the Worcestershire sauce. Over medium heat bring this mixture to a boil. Add the ketchup and stir until well-blended. Simmer over low heat for 30 minutes, stirring occasionally. Taste the sauce and adjust the seasonings to taste. This barbeque sauce can be refrigerated for up to a month. Makes about 1½ cups.

◆◆◆◆◆◆◆◆◆◆◆◆◆◆◆◆◆◆◆◆◆◆◆◆◆◆◆◆◆◆◆◆◆◆◆◆◆◆◆

Ginger & Hot Pepper Sauce

Fresh ginger is the exclamation point in this spicy oriental sauce.

◆ ◆ ◆

1/2 cup dry white wine

1/2 cup soy sauce

2 tablespoons honey

2 tablespoons rice wine vinegar

4 cloves garlic, minced

2 tablespoons fresh ginger, minced

1/8 teaspoon crushed hot pepper flakes

1 tablespoon cornstarch

3 tablespoons cold water

◆ ◆ ◆

In a small saucepan, combine the wine, soy sauce, honey, rice wine vinegar, garlic, ginger and the hot pepper flakes stirring to blend. Over medium-high heat, bring these to a boil. Reduce the heat to medium low and simmer uncovered for 10 minutes. In a small bowl, mix together the cornstarch and the water. When the sauce is done simmering, add the cornstarch mixture and cook, stirring, for 1 minute until the sauce is thickened. Refrigerate for up to a week. Makes about 1¼ cups.

◆◆◆◆◆◆◆◆◆◆◆◆◆◆◆◆◆◆◆◆◆◆◆◆◆◆◆◆◆◆◆◆◆◆◆◆◆

Latin-American Rib Sauce

Chipolte peppers in adobo sauce add a smoky and hot flavor to this rib sauce. You may substitute 1 tablespoon chili powder stirred into 2 tablespoons ketchup for the peppers.

◆ ◆ ◆

1 tablespoon vegetable oil

4 cloves garlic, minced

3 1/2 cups crushed tomatoes in puree

1/4 cup brown sugar, firmly packed

1/4 cup molasses

1/2 cup beer

1/4 cup cider vinegar

2 tablespoons Worcestershire sauce

2 tablespoons chipotles in adobo sauce

1/2 teaspoon ground cloves

1 teaspoon ground cinnamon

◆ ◆ ◆

In a large saucepan over medium heat, lightly brown the minced garlic in the heated oil. Add the tomatoes, brown sugar, molasses, beer, vinegar and the Worcestershire sauce, whisking to blend well. Add the chipotles, cloves and the cinnamon. Whisk to combine. Bring the sauce to a boil and reduce the heat to low. Simmer, uncovered until the sauce is thickened, about 30 minutes. The sauce can be refrigerated for up to a month. Makes about 4 cups.

Smokey-the-Bear Sauce

Grilled meat, barbeque sauce and that smoky smell in the air is a happy reminder of the great outdoors.

◆ ◆ ◆

1 tablespoon vegetable oil

1 medium onion, chopped

2 cloves garlic, minced

1 tablespoon chili powder

1 tablespoon molasses

3/4 cup beef broth

1/2 cup ketchup

1/2 cup bottled chili sauce

1/4 cup cider vinegar

1 tablespoon Worcestershire sauce

1 1/2 teaspoons liquid smoke

1/2 teaspoon hot pepper sauce

◆ ◆ ◆

In a medium saucepan, heat the oil over medium heat and sauté the onion and garlic just until they are softened. Stir in the chili powder and heat and stir for 30 seconds. Add the molasses, beef broth, ketchup, chili sauce, vinegar, Worcestershire sauce and the liquid smoke and bring just to a boil. Reduce the heat to low and simmer, uncovered, for 25 minutes. Add the hot pepper sauce and stir to combine. This sauce can be refrigerated for a week. Makes about 2½ cups.

◆◆◆

Basil & Balsamic Vinegar Sauce

This is a perfect sauce for grilled vegetables or mild-flavored fish. The flavor is tangy, but not over-powering for the tender flavors of the grilled foods.

◆ ◆ ◆

1 cup balsamic vinegar

1/3 cup dry white wine

2 tablespoons honey

1 tablespoon olive oil

2 tablespoon fresh basil, chopped

2 tablespoon fresh parsley, chopped

2 teaspoons freshly ground black pepper

◆ ◆ ◆

In a small saucepan, combine the vinegar, white wine, honey, oil and half of the basil, parsley and black pepper. Over medium-high heat bring this to a boil, then reduce the heat to medium-low and simmer for 15 minutes. The sauce should thicken. Stir in the remaining basil, parsley and pepper. Brush this sauce on during the last 15 minutes of grilling. The sauce can be refrigerated for up to a week. Makes about 1 cup.

◆◆◆

Orange Mustard Sauce

The orange marmalade adds a sweetness to the sauce that richly complements seafood and pork.

◆ ◆ ◆

1/2 cup orange marmalade

1/2 cup Dijon mustard

1/3 cup fresh orange juice

1/4 cup dry white wine

1 teaspoon dried rosemary

1/2 teaspoon celery seed

1 teaspoon orange zest, grated

◆ ◆ ◆

In a small saucepan, combine the marmalade, mustard, orange juice, white wine, rosemary, celery seed and the orange zest. Over medium-low heat bring the sauce to a simmer, stirring often, until the sauce is slightly thickened, about 8 minutes. Brush the sauce on the meat during the last 10 minutes of grilling. The sauce can be refrigerated for a week. Makes about 1½ cups

◆◆◆◆◆◆◆◆◆◆◆◆◆◆◆◆◆◆◆◆◆◆◆◆◆◆◆◆◆◆◆◆◆◆◆◆◆◆◆

Pineapple Sweet & Sour Sauce

*This is an excellent dipping sauce for
chicken and shellfish, or use during the last
ten minutes of grilling. The pineapple
juice adds a touch of the exotic.*

◆ ◆ ◆

1 cup ketchup

1/2 cup white vinegar

1/2 cup molasses

1/4 cup pineapple juice

1 tablespoon soy sauce

1/2 teaspoon ground ginger

1/4 teaspoon cayenne pepper

◆ ◆ ◆

In a nonreactive saucepan, combine the ketchup,
vinegar, molasses, pineapple juice, soy sauce, ginger
and the cayenne pepper, mixing well. Over medium-
high heat, bring the mixture to a boil; reduce the heat
to low and simmer for 15 to 20 minutes. Stir
occasionally. The sauce can be refrigerated for a week.
Makes about 2 cups.

◆◆◆◆◆◆◆◆◆◆◆◆◆◆◆◆◆◆◆◆◆◆◆◆◆◆◆◆◆◆◆◆◆◆◆◆◆◆◆

◆◆◆◆◆◆◆◆◆◆◆◆◆◆◆◆◆◆◆◆◆◆◆◆◆◆◆◆◆◆◆◆◆◆◆◆◆◆

Cayenne Pepper Peanut Sauce

*Hot and spicy with a rich peanut flavor, this sauce
is perfect for dipping and grilling. Brush the sauce
on during the last 10 minutes of grilling, or use it
for dipping seafood, chicken and vegetables.*

◆ ◆ ◆

3 tablespoons peanut oil

1 cup onions, minced

2 cups chunky peanut butter

2 cups chicken broth

2 tablespoons brown sugar

2 tablespoons cider vinegar

1/2 teaspoon cayenne pepper

◆ ◆ ◆

In a medium saucepan, sauté the onions in the peanut
oil until they are soft. Add the peanut butter, chicken
broth, brown sugar, cider vinegar and the cayenne
pepper. Blend well. Over medium-low heat, simmer the
sauce for 10 to 15 minutes, stirring frequently to
prevent the sauce from sticking to the bottom of the
pan. This sauce can be the refrigerated for up to a week.
Makes about 2½ cups sauce.

◆◆◆◆◆◆◆◆◆◆◆◆◆◆◆◆◆◆◆◆◆◆◆◆◆◆◆◆◆◆◆◆◆◆◆◆◆◆

◆◆

Maple Spice Sauce

This sauce is especially good for grilled fruits and cakes. Brush this on bananas, pineapple, and pound cakes before and during grilling! It's delicious!

◆ ◆ ◆

1 cup maple syrup

2 tablespoons butter

2 1/2 tablespoons lemon juice

1 teaspoon ground cinnamon

1/2 teaspoon ground allspice

1/4 teaspoon ground nutmeg

1/4 teaspoon ground cloves

◆ ◆ ◆

In a small saucepan over medium heat, simmer the maple syrup for 10 minutes until it has reduced to about ¾ cup. Stir in the butter, let it melt and remove the saucepan from the heat. Cool. Stir in the lemon juice, cinnamon, allspice, nutmeg and the cloves, blending well. This sauce can be refrigerated for up to a week. To use, reheat the sauce to melt the butter. Makes about 1 cup.

◆◆

Garlic Lemon Caper Sauce

*Fresh lemon juice is the base for the
flavors of garlic and capers in this sauce.
Excellent with seafood or chicken.*

❖ ❖ ❖

1/2 cup fresh lemon juice

3 tablespoons extra-virgin olive oil

6 cloves garlic, minced

1/4 cup scallions, minced

1 tablespoon lemon zest

1 teaspoon ground black pepper

1/4 cup small capers, drained

❖ ❖ ❖

In a nonreactive bowl, whisk together the lemon juice
and the olive oil. Add and stir until well-blended the
garlic, scallions, lemon zest, black pepper and the
capers. Cover and refrigerate for at least 2 hours before
using. This sauce can be refrigerated for up to 4 days.
Makes about 1 cup.

Tangy Mustard Barbeque Sauce

Horseradish and vinegar combine in this sauce to produce a nuance of tangy goodness. Use this sauce on pork, or for finishing chicken and turkey during the last 30 minutes of grilling.

◆ ◆ ◆

12 oz. can tomato paste

3/4 cup white vinegar

1/2 cup water

1/2 cup prepared yellow mustard

1 tablespoon prepared horseradish

1/4 cup dark brown sugar, firmly packed

1/3 cup Worcestershire sauce

1 tablespoon butter

2 teaspoons ground black pepper

1 teaspoon garlic powder

1/2 teaspoon salt

1/4 teaspoon cayenne pepper

◆ ◆ ◆

Combine the tomato paste, vinegar, water, mustard, horseradish, brown sugar, Worcestershire sauce, butter, pepper, garlic powder, salt and the cayenne pepper in a large nonreactive saucepan. Over high heat, bring the mixture to a quick boil, stirring to blend well. Reduce the heat and simmer the sauce for 10 to 15 minutes. This sauce can be refrigerated for up to 3 weeks. Makes about 3 cups

◆◆◆◆◆◆◆◆◆◆◆◆◆◆◆◆◆◆◆◆◆◆◆◆◆◆◆◆◆◆◆◆◆◆◆◆◆

Tomato & Chile Salsa

Fresh tomatoes and cilantro are the basis for this wonderfully spicy salsa.

◆◆◆

2 cups ripe tomatoes, peeled, seeded and chopped

1 cup minced onion

1 tablespoon fresh lime juice

3 tablespoons fresh tomato juice

2 tablespoons fresh cilantro, minced

1 tablespoon small green chilies, minced

2 cloves garlic, pressed

2 teaspoons chili powder

1 teaspoon ground black pepper

1/2 teaspoon salt

◆◆◆

In a nonreactive bowl, combine the tomatoes, onion, lime juice, tomato juice, cilantro, chilies, pressed garlic, chili powder, black pepper and the salt. Toss gently, cover and refrigerate for at least 2 hours to let the flavors mingle. Serve fresh. This salsa can be refrigerated for up to 3 days, but is best on the day that it is made. Makes about 3½ cups

◆◆◆◆◆◆◆◆◆◆◆◆◆◆◆◆◆◆◆◆◆◆◆◆◆◆◆◆◆◆◆◆◆◆◆◆◆

Jicama-Citrus Salsa

This salsa is light and tasty with a hint of heat.
Serve with fish or poultry.

❖ ❖ ❖

1 1/2 cup jicama, peeled and finely
   chopped
1 cup orange slices, finely chopped
1/4 cup fresh parsley, minced
1/4 cup fresh orange juice
1 tablespoon white vinegar
1 teaspoon jalapeño peppers, minced
1/2 teaspoon ground black pepper
1/2 teaspoon salt

❖ ❖ ❖

Combine the jicama, orange, parsley, orange juice, vinegar, jalapeño peppers, pepper, and the salt in a nonreactive bowl. Stir gently to blend. Cover and chill for at least 2 hours for flavors to blend. Refrigerate for up to 2 days. The salsa is best when served the day it is made. Makes about 3 cups.

Tomatillo Salsa Verde

*The tomatillos and chilies create the green color
of this salsa. It is spicy and flavorful.*

❖❖❖

1 1/2 cups tomatillos, chopped

1/4 cup white onion, chopped

2 tablespoons serrano chile, seeded and
   diced

1 tablespoon fresh cilantro, minced

2 tablespoons fresh parsley, minced

3 cloves garlic, pressed

1/2 teaspoon salt

1 teaspoon ground black pepper

1/2 teaspoon crushed red pepper

2 tablespoons white vinegar

2 tablespoons water

❖❖❖

Using a food processor or blender, place the tomatillos,
onion, chile, cilantro, parsley, garlic, salt, black pepper,
red pepper and the vinegar into the bowl. Purée the
mixture, adding the water a little at a time. Adjust the
seasonings to taste and let it stand for at least 1 hour. The
salsa may be refrigerated for up to 3 days. It tastes best
when served on the day it was made. Makes about 2 cups.

Pineapple Peach Salsa

Pineapple and peaches in a salsa are unusual, but not when grilling fruit or mild fish. Try it on top of grilled mahi-mahi or a golden grilled banana.

❖ ❖ ❖

1 cup fresh pineapple, finely chopped

1 cup fresh peach, peeled and chopped

2 tablespoons green onion, finely chopped

2 tablespoons pineapple juice

1/4 cup white wine vinegar

1/4 cup honey

2 tablespoons fresh parsley, minced

1 clove garlic, pressed

1/2 teaspoon salt

❖ ❖ ❖

Combine the pineapple, peaches, green onion, pineapple juice, white wine vinegar, honey, parsley, garlic and salt, gently stirring to blend well. Cover the bowl and refrigerate for at least 2 hours. Best when served on the day this salsa was made. It can be refrigerated for up to 2 days. Makes about 2½ cups

MaryAnn's Garden Tomato Salsa

The fresh vegetables and tomatoes mingle together in this salsa. It works well beside a grilled vegetable or on a hamburger patty.

◆ ◆ ◆

1 pound ripe plum tomatoes, seeded and chopped

1/2 cup white onions, diced

1/2 cup celery, diced

1/2 cup green bell pepper, diced

1/2 cup cucumber, peeled and diced

1/4 cup fresh basil, minced

3 tablespoons fresh parsley, minced

3 tablespoons extra-virgin olive oil

3 tablespoons balsamic vinegar

1 tablespoon Dijon mustard

2 cloves garlic, pressed

1/2 teaspoon ground black pepper

◆ ◆ ◆

In a nonreactive bowl, combine the tomatoes, onions, celery, bell pepper, cucumber, basil, parsley, olive oil, balsamic vinegar, mustard, garlic and the ground black pepper. Toss gently to mix well. Cover and refrigerate for 2 hours until the flavors have combined. The flavor is the best when served the day this salsa was made. Refrigerate for up to 2 days if needed. Makes about 3½ cups.

Texas Everything-Inside Salsa

Black-eyed peas are the tasty backbone of this warm peppery salsa. Spoon it over grilled steaks or on top of green salads.

◆ ◆ ◆

1/4 cup bacon, diced

1/4 cup red onion, diced

2 cloves garlic, pressed

1 cup green bell pepper, diced

2 cups black-eyed peas, cooked and drained, or canned

2 tablespoons olive oil

1/4 cup tomato juice

2 tablespoons water

1/4 cup fresh parsley, chopped

1/2 teaspoon crushed red pepper

1 teaspoon ground black pepper

1/2 cup tomatoes, peeled, seeded and diced

◆ ◆ ◆

In a nonreactive saucepan, brown the bacon until it is crisp. Remove the bacon and set aside. Add to the bacon grease the onion, garlic, green pepper and the black-eyed peas and sauté until tender, about 5 minutes. Add the oil, tomato juice, water, parsley, red pepper and the black pepper. Cook for another 3 minutes. Reduce the heat and add the tomatoes and crisp bacon. Simmer over low heat for 10 minutes. Serve warm or chilled. The salsa can be refrigerated for up to 5 days. Makes about 3½ cups.

Black Bean & Corn Salsa

The color and flavor combination of this salsa is perfect for grilled pork and blackened fish. It can also be used as an accompaniment to a main meal.

◆ ◆ ◆

16 ounce can black beans, rinsed and drained

9 ounce frozen corn kernels, thawed and drained

1 cup ripe tomatoes, chopped

1/2 cup white onions, diced

1/4 cup green bell pepper, minced

1/4 cup balsamic vinegar

2 tablespoons fresh parsley, minced

1 tablespoon fresh cilantro, minced

2 teaspoons hot sauce

2 cloves garlic, pressed

1 teaspoon chili powder

1/2 teaspoon ground black pepper

1/2 teaspoon salt

1/3 cup vegetable oil

◆ ◆ ◆

In a nonreactive bowl, combine the beans, corn, tomatoes, onions and the bell pepper. Set aside. In a small bowl, whisk together thoroughly the vinegar, parsley, cilantro, hot sauce, garlic, chili powder, black pepper and the salt. Add the vegetable oil a little at a time and whisk after each addition until the mixture is well-blended. Pour this over the bean mixture and toss to coat. Cover and refrigerate for at least 2 hours before serving. The salsa can be refrigerated for up to 3 days. Makes about 5 cups.

Tropical Mango & Papaya Salsa

*Tropical fruits, a touch of coconut and
a hint of spicy pepper combine together
in this delectable salsa.*

◆ ◆ ◆

1 cup ripe mango, peeled, seeded and diced

1 cup ripe papaya, peeled, seeded and
   diced

1/4 cup shredded coconut

1/2 cup pineapple juice

2 teaspoons fresh cilantro, minced

2 teaspoons crushed red pepper

1 tablespoon dry white wine

◆ ◆ ◆

In a nonreactive bowl, combine the mango, papaya,
coconut, pineapple juice, cilantro, red pepper and the
white wine. Toss gently to combine thoroughly. Cover
and refrigerate for at least 2 hours before serving. This
salsa can be refrigerated for up to 3 days. Makes about
2½ cups.

Red Onion Salsa

*Sautéed red onions lightly sprinkled with
rosemary bring a unique adaptation to salsa.
Serve this warm over beef or pork.*

◆ ◆ ◆

2 teaspoons extra-virgin olive oil

5 cups red onions, slivered

1 teaspoon sugar

2 teaspoons red wine vinegar

2 tablespoons fresh rosemary, lightly diced

2 teaspoons fresh parsley, minced

1/4 teaspoon ground black pepper

1/4 teaspoon salt

◆ ◆ ◆

Over medium-high heat, sauté the slivered red onions
in the olive oil until they are lightly browned. Reduce
the heat to medium and add the sugar, red wine
vinegar, rosemary, parsley, black pepper and the salt.
Simmer, stirring occasionally, for 5 minutes. Serve
warm or at room temperature. The salsa can be
refrigerated for up to 4 days, but is best when served
immediately. Makes about 4½ cups.

Teriyaki Mustard Marinade

*Soy sauce and mustard are the
basic flavors of this tangy marinade.
It works best on beef or pork.*

❖ ❖ ❖

1/2 cup soy sauce

1/2 cup vegetable oil

3 tablespoons honey

3 tablespoons prepared mustard

1/4 cup rice wine vinegar

1/4 teaspoon ground black pepper

1 clove garlic, pressed

1/2 cup green onion, minced

❖ ❖ ❖

In a small bowl, whisk together the soy sauce, vegetable oil, honey, mustard and the rice wine vinegar until well-blended. Stir in the black pepper, garlic and the green onion. Place the meat in a shallow nonreactive container and pour this marinade over the meat. Turn the meat to coat. Cover and refrigerate for about 4 hours, turning the meat occasionally. Marinate chicken for 2 hours; marinate fish for 1 hour. Makes about 1½ cups.

Rum & Molasses Marinade

*Dark and sweet in flavor, this marinade
is great for the thicker cuts of beef.*

◆ ◆ ◆

1/2 cup cider vinegar

1/3 cup dark molasses

1/2 cup vegetable oil

1/4 cup rum

1/4 teaspoon ground black pepper

1 clove garlic, minced

1 tablespoon fresh parsley, minced

◆ ◆ ◆

In a small bowl, whisk together the vinegar, molasses, oil and the rum until smooth and well-blended. Stir in the black pepper, garlic and the parsley. Place the meat in a shallow dish and pour the marinade over the meat. Turn the meat once and cover it. Refrigerate for at least 5 hours or overnight. Turn the meat occasionally. Makes about 1½ cups.

Delicate Herb Marinade

Mild tender fish fillets are enhanced with a light-flavored marinade. This is a marinade that complements the gentleness of seafood.

◆ ◆ ◆

1/2 cup rice wine vinegar

1/4 cup fresh lemon juice

2 tablespoons vegetable oil

2 teaspoons lemon zest

1 tablespoon fresh basil, minced

1 tablespoon fresh parsley, minced

1 tablespoon fresh thyme, minced

1/4 teaspoon ground black pepper

◆ ◆ ◆

In a small bowl, whisk together the vinegar, lemon juice and the oil until smooth and blended. Add the zest, basil, parsley, thyme and the black pepper and stir to mix well. Pour this over the seafood that has been placed in a shallow glass dish. Turn the seafood once, cover the dish and refrigerate for about 30 minutes. Turn the seafood occasionally as it marinates. Marinate pork for 1 to 2 hours. Makes about 1 cup.

Island Marinade

*A little curry, some ginger, cinnamon and cloves
fill this with the flavor of the islands.*

◆ ◆ ◆

1 cup soy sauce

1/2 cup honey

1/4 cup fresh lime juice

1 teaspoon ground ginger

3 cloves garlic, minced

1 teaspoon curry powder

1 teaspoon salt

1/2 teaspoon ground cinnamon

1/2 teaspoon ground cloves

◆ ◆ ◆

In a nonreactive bowl, whisk together the soy sauce, honey and the lime juice. Add and whisk thoroughly the ginger, garlic, curry powder, salt, cinnamon and the cloves. Place the meat in a shallow glass dish and pour this marinade over the meat. Turn the meat once, cover it and refrigerate. Turn meat occasionally as it marinates. Marinate beef steak for 2 to 4 hours, pork ribs for 3 to 5 hours, or chicken for 2 to 4 hours. Makes about 1¾ cups.

Five-Spice Chinese Marinade

Five-spice is a powder mix that you can find in the oriental section of your grocers or in a specialty food store.

◆ ◆ ◆

1/2 cup sugar

3 tablespoons sweet sherry

2 tablespoons soy sauce

1/2 cup hoisin sauce

1 teaspoon ground ginger

1/2 teaspoon five-spice powder

1 teaspoon salt

◆ ◆ ◆

In a nonreactive bowl, whisk together the sugar, sherry and soy sauce until the sugar dissolves. Add the hoisin sauce, ginger, five-spice powder and the salt. Blend well. Place the meat in a shallow dish and pour the marinade over the meat. Turn the meat once, cover and refrigerate. Turn the meat occasionally while it marinates. Marinate pork ribs for 2 to 4 hours and chicken 2 to 3 hours. Makes about 1½ cups.

Spicy Onion Marinade

*Only beef and pork can handle the
intense onion flavor in this marinade. Try it
with a beef brisket or a pork shoulder.*

❖ ❖ ❖

1/2 cup white vinegar

3 tablespoons grated onion

1 tablespoon onion powder

1 tablespoon dry mustard powder

1 teaspoon garlic powder

1/4 teaspoon crushed red pepper

1/4 teaspoon ground black pepper

1/2 cup vegetable oil

❖ ❖ ❖

In a nonreactive bowl, combine the vinegar and the grated onion. Whisk in the onion powder, dry mustard, garlic powder, red pepper and the black pepper until smooth. Add the oil and whisk until well-blended. Place the meat in a shallow baking dish and pour the marinade over the meat. Turn the meat once and cover. Refrigerate, turning the meat occasionally as it marinates. Marinate beef for 5 to 7 hours and the pork for 4 to 6 hours. Makes 1½ cups.

Southwestern Marinade

*Tomato juice, lime juice and minced
chilies give this a fiery flavor. The barbequed
meat can be shredded and used in tacos.*

❖ ❖ ❖

2 cups tomato juice

1/2 cup fresh lime juice

2 tablespoons dark brown sugar

1 tablespoon steak sauce

2 teaspoons chili powder

1 teaspoon ground cumin

2 teaspoons chipolte peppers, minced

1/2 teaspoon salt

❖ ❖ ❖

In a nonreactive bowl, whisk together the tomato juice,
lime juice, brown sugar, steak sauce, chili powder,
cumin, chipolte peppers and the salt until well-blended.
Place the meat in a shallow glass dish and pour the
marinade over the meat. Turn the meat once and cover.
Refrigerate to marinate, turning the meat occasionally.
Marinate pork for 3 to 5 hours, or beef for 4 to 6 hours.
Makes about 2½ cups.

Snappy Fresh Citrus Marinade

*This marinade is full of flavor combinations
that go well with chicken, fish and pork.*

◆ ◆ ◆

5 cloves garlic

1/2 teaspoon salt

2 teaspoons dried oregano

1/2 teaspoon ground cumin

1/3 cup red wine vinegar

1/3 cup fresh orange juice

1/3 cup fresh lime juice

2 tablespoons vegetable oil

1/4 cup fresh parsley, minced

1/4 teaspoon ground black pepper

◆ ◆ ◆

Mash the garlic with the salt to make a paste. Scrape this
into a small bowl and stir in the oregano and the cumin.
Blend well. Whisk in the vinegar, orange juice, lime juice,
vegetable oil, parsley and the black pepper until
completely mixed. Place the meat in a shallow baking
dish and pour the marinade over the meat. Turn the meat
once and cover the dish. Refrigerate while marinating the
meat. Marinate 30 minutes to 1 hour for fish and 1 to 2
hours for chicken or pork. Makes about 1 cup.